# MONEY WELL PLACED

## CHOOSE YOUR INVESTMENTS BASED ON ECONOMIC CONDITIONS AND TIME HORIZON

# MONEY WELL PLACED

## CHOOSE YOUR INVESTMENTS BASED ON ECONOMIC CONDITIONS AND TIME HORIZON

NATHANAEL POUZIN

# FULL TEXT

English version

—

First Edition

paper version
ISBN : 978-2-9597550-4-0 I EAN : 9782959755040

Paris, December 2025.

# TABLE OF CONTENTS

# INTRODUCTION

*M*ost people spend years learning how to earn money. Far fewer spend time learning what to do with it once they have it. We are told to save. We hear that real estate builds wealth. We are encouraged to invest in the stock market. Every day brings new advice, new opportunities, and new trends. The options seem endless, yet deciding where to put your money is often surprisingly difficult. Not because there are too few choices, but because there are so many. The question itself is simple: where should you invest your money?

The answer is less straightforward. There is no perfect investment. There are only investments that are appropriate—or inappropriate—for a particular goal, situation, and time horizon.

A savings account, for example, is an excellent place to keep money you may need within the next few months. It is a poor tool for building wealth over the next thirty years. Conversely, stocks have historically been one of the most effective ways to grow wealth over long periods, but they can become a costly choice if you need access to that money in the near future. The problem is rarely the investment itself. More often, the problem is a mismatch between the investment and the purpose it is meant to serve.

Every asset represents an underlying economic reality: a business generating profits, a government issuing debt, a piece of land, a stream of income, or a scarce resource. Understanding that reality is essential because it explains where an asset's value comes from and why investors expect it to produce returns. In this book, we will explore the major asset classes: cash, bonds, real estate, commodities, stocks, and cryptocurrencies. The objective is not to tell you what to buy. Instead, it is to help you understand how these assets work, what returns they have historically delivered, what risks they involve, and the time horizons over which they tend to perform best. Some assets are well suited to preserving capital. Others are designed to generate income or long-term growth. Each has strengths, weaknesses, and specific situations in which it can be useful—or harmful.

This book is not about finding the next hot investment. It does not promote any financial product, strategy, or institution. Its purpose is to give you the knowledge needed to think independently, evaluate opportunities rationally, and make decisions based on your own circumstances. The ultimate goal is simple: to help you build a portfolio that reflects your objectives, supports your long-term financial future, and avoids the mistakes that tend to be the most expensive over time.

# PART I

## The framework : Why every dollar needs a purpose

# CHAPTER 1:

## How money works for you

*E*very financial decision begins with the same thing: the money you have. We will not spend much time discussing how that money was earned. Some people build businesses, others work traditional jobs, inherit wealth, or follow entirely different paths. The details vary, but the starting point is always the same. Before investing, before asset allocation, and before financial markets, there is a simpler reality: how much money comes in, how much goes out, and how much remains. In other words, every person faces the same three variables: income, spending, and savings.

**Every dollar you earn must eventually go somewhere. It can be spent, saved, or invested.** At first glance, that may seem obvious. Yet most financial outcomes are determined by how consistently you make that choice over time. The question is simple: what should I do with my money today? The answer to that question shapes much of your financial future. Whether you become financially secure, remain dependent on your next paycheck, or build substantial wealth often comes down to how you divide your money between present consumption and future opportunities.

Spending provides an immediate benefit. It allows you to enjoy life today through housing, food, travel, entertainment, education, or countless other purchases. Spending is not inherently good or bad—it is simply the exchange of money for something you value in the present. Once the money is spent, however, it no longer belongs to you. Its financial value has been converted into immediate consumption. Investing follows a different logic. When you invest, you choose to postpone part of today's consumption in exchange for the possibility of greater opportunities tomorrow. Rather than spending your money now, you put it to work. You buy an asset that you expect to produce income, appreciate in value, or both. At its core, investing is an act of patience. It is the decision to sacrifice a portion of today's purchasing power in the hope of increasing your future purchasing power. Instead of consuming your capital, you give it the opportunity to grow.

Some uses of money do not fit neatly into a single category. A car, for example, may be used to commute to work, transport a family, or generate income through a business. The difference is not defined by the object itself but by the role it plays in your life. What matters is not what you buy, but how that purchase affects your future financial position.

Savings occupy a different place altogether. They sit between spending and investing. Unlike spending, the money is not consumed. Unlike investing, it is not exposed to meaningful risk in pursuit of higher returns. Instead, it remains available, waiting for a future need or opportunity. Think of savings as financial breathing room. Its purpose is not to make you rich. Its purpose is to keep you resilient. Savings allow you to absorb life's inevitable surprises: a job loss, an unexpected medical bill, a major home repair, or a temporary drop in income. They provide stability when circumstances become uncertain and flexibility when opportunities appear. Without savings, even a small setback can force difficult financial decisions. With savings, temporary problems are more likely to remain temporary. Many investors spend enormous amounts of time thinking about market risk while paying far less attention to a more immediate danger: life risk.

Life risk has nothing to do with stock prices. It comes from the unexpected events that disrupt everyday life. A lost job, a health issue, a broken roof, a failed business venture, or a sudden family expense can all place pressure on your finances regardless of what markets are doing. When these events occur, liquidity matters. Without sufficient cash reserves, you may be forced to sell investments at exactly the wrong time—not because the investment thesis has changed, but because you need the money. Markets do not care whether your timing is convenient.

This is why two investors with identical portfolios can experience very different outcomes. One has the financial flexibility to wait through difficult periods. The other is forced to sell when prices are depressed. The difference is rarely intelligence or investment skill. More often, it is preparation. Before seeking higher returns, you must first build a strong financial foundation. Without one, even the best investment strategy can fail when real life intervenes. That is the role of an emergency fund. It is often overlooked because it produces little return and appears to do nothing. Yet its value is revealed precisely when things go wrong. An emergency fund is not designed to grow your wealth. It is designed to protect it. After all, no one builds a cathedral by focusing on the roof while ignoring the foundation.

**The purpose of an emergency fund is not to make money. Its purpose is to protect your freedom of action.** When life becomes unpredictable, cash gives you options. It allows you to handle unexpected expenses, navigate periods of uncertainty, and avoid making financial decisions under pressure.

This is why an emergency fund is often more valuable than it appears. Its return is not measured in interest earned. Its return comes from the mistakes it helps you avoid. As Warren Buffett famously said, "Rule number one: never lose money. Rule number two: never forget rule number one." Before focusing on growing your wealth, your first objective should be to protect it. An emergency reserve helps you do exactly that by creating a margin of safety between you and life's inevitable surprises.A common rule of thumb is to keep enough readily accessible cash to cover six to twelve months of living expenses. Depending on your circumstances, a larger reserve may be appropriate. The goal is not precision. The goal is resilience. For entrepreneurs, freelancers, and anyone whose income fluctuates significantly, a larger emergency fund often makes sense. Income can decline suddenly or disappear altogether, while access to credit tends to become more difficult at the exact moment it is most needed. The same logic applies to retirees and investors who depend on their portfolios to generate income. Maintaining a sufficient cash reserve reduces the risk of having to sell investments during a market downturn simply to cover everyday expenses.

**Not all money has the same job. Some money is meant to protect you. Some money is meant to grow. Confusing the two is one of the most common causes of financial mistakes.** Money that may be needed in the near future should remain safe and accessible. Money that will not be needed for many years can afford to take greater risks in pursuit of higher returns.

A sound financial plan recognizes both realities. It provides enough security to withstand short-term challenges while allowing long-term capital the time it needs to compound and grow. This distinction is more important than many investors realize.

One of the most common investing mistakes is placing short-term money into long-term investments and then being forced to sell before the investment thesis has had time to play out. Equally common is leaving long-term capital sitting in low-return accounts where inflation quietly erodes its purchasing power year after year. In both cases, the problem is not the investment itself. The problem is that the money was given the wrong job.

# CHAPTER 2:

## The role of psychology in investment

*I*nvesting is, at its core, a trade-off. You give up some spending today in the hope of having more spending power tomorrow. But investing does not create wealth out of thin air. It simply moves resources through time. You sacrifice certainty in the present for the possibility of greater rewards in the future. The challenge is that the future is uncertain. No one knows exactly what the economy will look like in ten years. No one knows which companies will dominate their industries, what interest rates will be, or how markets will behave. Every investment therefore contains an element of uncertainty. In that sense, investing always requires a degree of faith. That is why expectations matter.

As Howard Marks explains in *The Most Important Thing*, there are very few investments that are inherently good or bad. What matters is the price you pay, the risks you assume, and the time horizon over which you evaluate the outcome. An asset can be a terrible investment over two years and an excellent investment over twenty. Many investors make the mistake of judging long-term decisions using short-term results. They become disappointed when reality fails to match their expectations, even when the investment is behaving exactly as it should. Understanding the natural time horizon of an asset is therefore essential. It helps you develop realistic expectations and gives your investment strategy the time it needs to work.

Yet knowledge alone is rarely enough. Even when investors understand the logic of long-term investing, living through periods of uncertainty can be emotionally difficult. Markets rarely move in a straight line. There will be setbacks, disappointments, and periods when doing nothing feels almost impossible. This is where psychology becomes more important than finance.

The emotional challenge of investing is often less visible in real estate than in financial markets. Property prices move more slowly, transactions are infrequent, and daily fluctuations are largely hidden from view. But the psychology is the same. In 2003, near the peak of the American housing boom, most households believed it was a good time to buy real estate. A few years later, the housing market collapsed and triggered one of the most severe financial crises in modern history. The lesson is timeless: when everyone feels comfortable, risk is often higher than it appears. When fear is widespread, opportunities are often closer than they seem.

Financial markets make these emotional swings even harder to ignore because prices are visible every day.

When markets rise, optimism grows. Investors become more confident. Sometimes they become too confident. Recent gains begin to feel permanent, and risks that once seemed unacceptable suddenly appear reasonable. When markets fall, the opposite happens. Confidence turns into doubt. Doubt turns into fear. Investors abandon long-term plans, change strategies at the worst possible moment, and sell assets they previously had every intention of holding. The cycle is as old as investing itself.

This is why successful investing is often less about intelligence than about temperament.

The best investors learn to remain disciplined when others become emotional. They understand that markets will fluctuate, headlines will change, and periods of uncertainty are unavoidable. Rather than reacting to every movement, they focus on the long-term process. As Warren Buffett famously said, "The stock market is a device for transferring money from the impatient to the patient." As a result, two investors can own exactly the same assets and achieve entirely different outcomes. The reason is simple: investing is not merely a technical exercise. It is deeply psychological.

Most investment mistakes are not caused by markets. They are caused by investors reacting to markets under pressure creating a gap of about 1.5% to 3% per year (Dalbar, *Quantitative Analysis of Investor Behavior*, 2023)[1]. Panic selling during downturns, chasing performance after prices have already soared, or constantly switching strategies in search of something better—these decisions often do far more damage than any market correction ever could. For that reason, the best investment strategy is not necessarily the one that looks best on a spreadsheet. It is the one you can stick with consistently through both good times and bad. A strategy that makes you panic during every downturn is not a good strategy for you, regardless of how strong its historical returns may appear.

Knowing yourself is therefore one of the most valuable investing skills you can develop. How much volatility can you truly tolerate? How will you react when your portfolio loses 20 percent of its value? How long can you remain patient when results fail to meet expectations? These questions matter because successful investing is not simply about predicting the future. It is about managing your own behavior while the future unfolds.

By now, several important principles should be clear. **Without a financial safety net, you are vulnerable. Without a clear time horizon, you are exposed. And without emotional discipline, you risk selling at precisely the moment when patience is needed most.**

# CHAPTER 3 :

## Measuring what matters: performance, risk, and time horizon

*B*efore deciding where to invest, you need a way to evaluate the opportunities in front of you. This chapter introduces a few simple concepts that will help us compare assets throughout the rest of the book.

At first glance, investments can look completely different. A share of stock, a rental property, a government bond, a gold bar, or a cryptocurrency may seem to have little in common. Yet they all share one important characteristic: their value is ultimately measured in money. You might own a house, a portfolio of stocks, or a quantity of gold, but when you evaluate your wealth, you almost always translate those assets into a common unit of account. In everyday life, that unit is typically your local currency. In global finance, it is often the U.S. dollar. Ultimately, what matters is not how many shares, ounces, or coins you own. What matters is the purchasing power those assets provide. A portfolio worth $1 million gives you more options than one worth $500,000, regardless of the assets it contains. From that perspective, investing is simply the process of increasing future purchasing power.

The challenge is that the future is uncertain.

Every investment involves a range of possible outcomes. Some will be favorable. Others will not. Good investing therefore requires thinking in probabilities rather than certainties. One useful concept is expected return. Expected return is not a prediction. It is an estimate of the average outcome you might reasonably expect when different possibilities are weighted by their likelihood. Imagine a one-year loan. You estimate a 5% chance of losing your entire investment and a 95% chance of earning 10%. The expected return is therefore: (5% × 0%) + (95% × 110%) = 4.5% per year. This is not a guaranteed return; it is an expectation. And that distinction is essential. The same logic applies to any investment. Risk is almost always present. It is not an exception but a condition of investing. It is the price you pay for the possibility of future return, and it must therefore be measured rather than ignored.

This way of thinking changes how you evaluate opportunities. It forces you to consider both upside and downside, weighted by their probabilities. An asset with high potential returns but a significant probability of loss may end up with a lower expected return than a more modest but stable investment. Historical returns tell you what has already happened. Expected returns help you understand what is reasonably likely to happen next.

That said, higher returns often come with greater fluctuations, uncertainty, and short-term losses. A 4.5% return achieved through constant volatility and emotional stress is very different from the same 4.5% earned steadily and calmly. The outcome may be identical on paper, but the investor experience is not. This is precisely what the Sharpe ratio—named after the American economist William Sharpe—attempts to capture. It measures the excess return of an asset relative to the risk-free rate, adjusted for volatility. In other words, it evaluates efficiency: how much return you are receiving for each unit of risk taken. The goal is not simply to maximize returns, but to maximize returns per unit of risk.

From this perspective, investing becomes a matter of assigning a time horizon to each unit of money you save, and allocating it accordingly based on the level of risk it can reasonably support. Investing is ultimately about positioning your money to be worth more in the future than it is today. But how you achieve that matters.

But there is one more variable that matters just as much: price. Even the best asset can become a poor investment if purchased at an unreasonable price. The price you pay today has a significant influence on the return you ultimately earn tomorrow. This is why valuation matters. Successful investing is not simply about finding good assets. It is about acquiring good assets at sensible prices and holding them long enough for their value to emerge.

In the end, investing is less about prediction than preparation. It is about preparing for uncertainty, surviving inevitable setbacks, and remaining positioned to benefit when opportunities arise. The better you understand risk, return, time, and valuation, the better equipped you will be to navigate the cycles that every investor eventually faces.

A well-constructed portfolio is about balance. It combines different asset classes—cash, bonds, commodities, real estate, equities, and increasingly, cryptocurrencies—each playing a different role. The question is not whether to use all of them, but why you would mix them in the first place. Because saving alone is not enough. Holding cash feels safe. It creates a sense of stability, and on the surface, it looks like progress. The number in your account does not go down, and that can be reassuring. But this sense of security is often misleading. Over time, cash does not reliably preserve purchasing power against its silent enemy: inflation. Inflation does not reduce the nominal amount of money you hold. Your balance stays the same. Instead, it slowly reduces what that money can buy. What costs $1,000 today will cost more tomorrow, and even more in the years ahead. In that sense, saving is often about preserving a number, not preserving value. If your money is not earning a return, it is quietly losing purchasing power. This creates a difficult trade-off. Too much cash leaves you exposed to inflation. Too little cash leaves you vulnerable to short-term shocks. The challenge is finding the right balance between safety and efficiency. Here are some examples:

- You have a 60/40 portfolio composed of 60% equities and 40% bonds. This is the historical model used by institutional investors[2]. In a simple model, stocks provide growth, and bonds the necessary cushioning during times of crisis. Because our needs change over time (family situation, age), the older we get, the less we can wait for an upward cycle or "recover" our losses. Therefore, the proportion allocated to bonds should be significant (30% at age 30, 80% at age 80, for example).
- The *Permanent Portfolio* of Harry Browne. Very simple, it is composed of 25% stocks; 25% long-term bonds; 25% gold (to protect against an inflationary scenario); and 25% cash (to protect against scenarios of falling inflation and/or recession) ;
- The *All Weather Portfolio* by Ray Dalio (founder of the Bridgewater Associates fund[3]). This portfolio was designed to withstand all economic cycles. Simply put, it consists of four balanced blocks of 25% each, presenting the same level of risk and each responding to a specific scenario: (1) rising inflation (inflation-linked bonds, emerging market credit, commodities); (2) lower inflation (equities, nominal bonds); (3) higher growth (equities, corporate credit, emerging market credit, commodities); and (4) lower growth than expected (traditional bonds[4], inflation-linked bonds). The idea is to make the portfolio resilient to all economic scenarios, since they cannot be predicted precisely.

First, it is important **to recognize that holding cash is simply one investment choice among others.** As we have seen, every dollar you own can be spent, invested, or saved. In that sense, saving is not the absence of an investment decision—it is a decision in itself. **It means allocating money to an asset that offers maximum liquidity and virtually no risk of capital loss,** in exchange for very little or no return.

Second, that there is no single correct answer. Although many studies attempt to define an "optimal" portfolio, no universal allocation exists. The right mix of assets depends on your time horizon, your objectives, and your tolerance for risk. In other words, portfolio construction is not about finding the perfect formula. It is about finding a structure that fits with your reality.

The portfolio examples we have discussed also share a common philosophy: none of them is designed to maximize returns at any cost. Instead, each is built to remain functional through unpredictable economic cycles, without forcing the investor to sell at the worst possible moment. This is less a formula than a mindset: resilience matters more than optimization.

They also share an important limitation. All of these examples are purely financial portfolios. They exclude real assets such as real estate—and in particular the primary residence, which is often the largest source of wealth for households around the world. These models are therefore best seen as frameworks for thinking, not rigid templates to follow mechanically. If there is no single optimal portfolio, the question becomes more practical: Which one should you choose?
Or more precisely, how should you build your own? To answer this, we will now turn to the expected return of the main asset classes, based on their respective time horizons.

Before doing so, the next chapter will help you identify a few guiding principles—and, if needed, determine where to begin.

# CHAPTER 4:

## The decision map: a guide to reading this book

*T*his book can be read in two ways. You can follow it in chronological order to build a complete understanding of financial markets through a structured progression. Or you can use it as a more targeted guide, starting with the chapters that correspond to your current situation. Both approaches are valid. However, if you have a specific objective in mind, this chapter will help you decide where to begin. You can go directly to the section that concerns you most, and return to the other chapters later.

- If you do not yet have an emergency fund, your priority is the short term. The first step is to build a contingency reserve (see Part II) and eliminate non-interest-bearing debt. In many cases, borrowing costs are high and unnecessary, making debt reduction the most effective starting point;
- If you have savings available or anticipate significant expenses in the coming years—such as education, a down payment on a home, renovations, or a business acquisition—cash and short-term bonds are the most appropriate tools during this phase (see Parts II and IV);
- If you are considering a real estate investment, the key question is whether buying is superior to renting in your situation. This can be assessed by comparing the costs and benefits of both options and by estimating the internal rate of return (IRR) of the project based on your initial equity contribution (Part III);
- If you already own your primary residence and are

seeking long-term returns, a combination of bonds and equities may be appropriate (see Parts IV and VI), without excluding the possibility of additional real estate investments (see Part III);

- If you have chosen to remain a renter, equities become the primary tool for long-term wealth accumulation and retirement planning. In this case, exposure to precious metals can also be considered as a partial hedge against currency risk (see Parts V and VI), while keeping real estate as a potential option depending on future opportunities (see Part III);
- If you are concerned about high inflation, precious metals may provide protection—either as a full allocation in the event of a severe shock or as a partial hedge if the risk is more localized. In some cases, holding a strong foreign currency may also be relevant depending on your domestic environment. Real estate should also not be overlooked, particularly as a long-term hedge when financed with fixed-rate debt[5] (see Part III);
- If you have a higher risk tolerance, are willing to accept greater volatility, or are interested in exploring alternative investments such as cryptocurrencies, the dedicated section of the book (see Part VII) may be relevant once the foundational principles are understood.

For example, you might keep $10,000 aside as an emergency fund that you never intend to touch. Another $20,000 could be reserved for a goal you expect to fund within the next two years. The rest might be invested over a fifteen-year horizon. These three pools of capital follow completely different logics. They should not be managed in the same way.

Before moving on, it is worth pausing to think about your own situation. How many separate pools of money do you currently have? What time horizon does each one correspond to? And most importantly, how comfortable would you be if each of them temporarily fell by 20% or even 40% in value without forcing you to sell? This question matters because different asset classes behave very differently in the short and medium term. Some are relatively stable. Others can fluctuate significantly. In practice, your time horizon and your tolerance for volatility explain most of your asset allocation decisions.

While your current financial situation is more important than your age, life stage can still serve as a useful guide for making simple adjustments:

## You are young and just starting your career

You have time on your side. At this stage of life, the priority is simple: build a safety net, and begin investing for the long term, primarily in equities (see Parts II and VI). When you are young, you may not have much capital. But you have something far more valuable: time. In financial markets, time is what turns small, consistent decisions into meaningful outcomes. For example, investing $200 per month in index funds starting at age 25 can grow to roughly $528,000 by age 65, assuming an average annual return of 7%. If you start the same strategy at age 35, the result drops to about $245,000. A ten-year delay cuts the outcome nearly in half.

The lesson is straightforward: you do not need to wait until you have "enough" money to start investing. There is no meaningful minimum threshold. What matters far more than the amount is consistency over time. Investing $200 per month early in life is ultimately more powerful than investing $1,000 per month much later. Consistency matters more than size.

## Retirement is approaching

At this stage, the logic begins to change. You are no longer investing with a multi-decade horizon and the ability to recover from large market declines. The focus gradually shifts away from maximizing long-term growth toward preserving capital and managing risk. Equities still play a role, but they must be balanced with more stable assets such as bonds (see Part IV). A major market downturn at age 55, when your portfolio is fully exposed to equities, can create a difficult situation. The goal is therefore not to abandon growth, but to reduce the risk of being forced to sell risky assets at the wrong time. In practice, this usually means directing new contributions toward bonds first, and then progressively increasing the share of defensive assets as retirement approaches. Once retirement begins, the portfolio naturally transitions into a withdrawal phase. Assets such as precious metals—often accumulated earlier in life when they were less central to the strategy—may also play a complementary role (see Part V).

A key challenge in retirement planning is underestimating how much capital you will need, or how long you will live. The so-called 4% rule, introduced by William Bengen (Bengen, *Determining Withdrawal Rates Using Historical Data*, Journal of Financial Planning, 1994), suggests that a 4% annual withdrawal rate may allow a portfolio to last around 30 years under certain assumptions. The Trinity Study reaches similar conclusions, with sustainable withdrawal rates typically in the 3% to 4% range depending on portfolio composition and market conditions.

Between these two stages, other parts of the financial picture should not be ignored. Real estate holdings, for example, should be reviewed objectively and without emotional bias (see Part III). Liquidity also becomes more important than many investors expect (see Part II), especially as financial responsibilities often increase—children, family support, debt repayment —alongside unexpected expenses. Flexibility becomes essential. Your financial structure must be able to absorb these demands without forcing poor decisions.

Ultimately, **asset allocation is not static. It evolves with your life.** It should be reviewed regularly and adjusted when major changes occur—marriage, the birth of a child, job loss, inheritance, or retirement. A portfolio that does not evolve with its owner gradually becomes disconnected from reality.

# PART II

## Cash and foreign currency: When doing nothing is the best solution

# CHAPTER 5 :

## The role of cash in a portfolio

**Cash is the most commonly chosen form for precautionary savings.** It is also the only major asset class that is not directly exposed to short-term market fluctuations—which is precisely what makes it so powerful.

Cash and cash equivalents include anything that can be accessed immediately without loss of value: physical currency, checking accounts, and regulated savings accounts. In simple terms, it is money held in its most liquid form—available at any time to handle emergencies or take advantage of opportunities. But cash plays another, often overlooked role: it shapes behavior. By keeping part of your wealth in cash, you reduce the risk of panic-driven decisions, such as selling investments during a market downturn. Cash does not make you richer. Its purpose is different. It helps you avoid costly mistakes when pressure is high.

The return on cash is typically linked to central bank policy rates. This is often referred to as the risk-free rate, meaning it is considered virtually certain under normal conditions, regardless of short-term market movements. In practice, however, the return is usually modest—often only a few percentage points[6] per year—and slightly below the official policy rate, since banks retain a margin for operating costs. Financial institutions, after all, are not charities.

A common guideline is to **hold six to twelve months of living expenses in cash reserves, depending on your personal situation. Within that buffer, it is often suggested to keep one**

**to three months of expenses in a checking account, with the remainder held in savings accounts.**

Checking accounts offer maximum flexibility but very low returns. Savings accounts provide slightly higher yields while remaining safe and easily accessible. For very short time horizons—typically less than three months—there is often no better option than a high-yield savings account, particularly in the United States. It may be slightly less convenient than a checking account, but it offers a better balance between liquidity and return without sacrificing safety.

As your time horizon extends, however, your options expand—and so does your potential return, without necessarily increasing risk. As Shlomo Benartzi and Richard Thaler have pointed out[7], it is paradoxical to postpone consumption only to earn returns as low as 1% per year.

The lesson from history is simple: **beyond your emergency reserve, and in the absence of a short-term need, cash is rarely an efficient long-term investment. Because cash produces little or no real return, it struggles to preserve purchasing power over time.** Outside of periods of falling prices or deflation, it typically loses value in real terms as inflation gradually erodes what it can buy. Even if the nominal amount remains unchanged, its real purchasing power declines slowly but steadily. For this reason, the share of cash in a portfolio should be carefully aligned with actual needs—not convenience or habit. Holding too much cash means giving up exposure to assets that are more productive over the long run. That trade-off is the opportunity cost of liquidity.

## In which currency should I keep my cash?

To make the most of your savings, it is worth asking whether another currency could ever make sense for an emergency fund.

In theory, you could hold cash in different currencies. In practice, an emergency fund has a very specific role: it must be immediately accessible, stable, and free from the risk of capital loss. For that reason, the best currency is usually the one you already use in daily life. It avoids unnecessary friction such as conversion fees, as well as foreign exchange risk. Exchange rates fluctuate constantly, and those fluctuations can add an additional layer of uncertainty to money that is supposed to be reliable. For emergency savings, simplicity matters more than optimization. **Foreign currencies are generally better suited to diversification or long-term investment strategies than to short-term safety reserves.**

But this raises a deeper question. What happens when your local currency steadily loses purchasing power, or consistently weakens against others over time? At that point, the currency itself begins to lose one of its essential functions. A currency serves two core purposes. First, it is a unit of account: a common standard that allows you to measure and compare the value of goods and services. Second, it is a medium of exchange: a tool that allows transactions to happen without barter. When a currency fails to preserve its value over time, its effectiveness in both roles is weakened. Prices become harder to interpret in real terms, and holding money becomes less about stability and more about managing gradual erosion of purchasing power.

- Money is used to measure and compare the value of things. Whether it's prices, wages, debts, profits, or anything else, everything is expressed in the same common "language": this unit of account called currency. Examples include the US dollar (USD) in the United States, the Japanese yen (JPY), the British pound sterling (GBP) in the United Kingdom, the Australian dollar (AUD) in Australia, the Canadian dollar (CAD) in Canada, the Swiss franc (CHF) in Switzerland, and so on. There are just under 200 different currencies in the world today. Each country has its own currency. Its own “language”, unless it decides to share this sovereignty with one (or more) neighbors. The case of the euro (EUR), shared today by 21 states on the

European continent, is the most telling;

- In addition to being a unit of account, money serves to eliminate the need for bartering. It is a means of exchange. There's no need to find someone who wants exactly what you have in return. Money acts as a conduit. It promotes trade and facilitates the acquisition (and therefore the sale for the other party) of a good or service. Money is the instrument that connects everything within a single country, but also internationally. Thus, the currency of one country can be exchanged for that of another, in turn facilitating investment and the purchase of new goods or services.

A third key function of money is its role as a store of value. It allows purchasing power to be preserved over time. In other words, money can be held today and used in the future without immediately losing its usefulness. This function works well under normal conditions. But it breaks down when inflation becomes extreme. When prices rise rapidly, money stops preserving value in any meaningful sense. Holding cash becomes costly. People try to spend it as quickly as possible, expecting it to lose even more value tomorrow. Confidence in the currency collapses. Businesses and households no longer want to hold it, and the system begins to shift away from money as we normally understand it. In such situations, barter or alternative currencies often reappear.

This extreme situation is known as hyperinflation. It occurred in the Weimar Republic in Germany[8] between 1921 and 1923, and more recently in Zimbabwe in the 2000s. When the store-of-value function fails, the other two roles of money—as a unit of account and as a medium of exchange—also become unstable. Prices lose meaning, contracts become difficult to structure, and economic activity becomes harder to coordinate. The result is usually either a partial return to barter or a shift toward more stable foreign currencies. In many cases, this leads to "dollarization": the replacement of a local currency with a stronger one, most often the US dollar, which continues to fulfill the basic functions of money. In Zimbabwe, for example, the complete abandonment of the Zimbabwean dollar in 2009 in favor of the US dollar (USD), and at times the South African rand (ZAR), was a policy response designed to stop hyperinflation and restore economic stability.

Under normal conditions, the situation is very different. When the interest earned on savings roughly offsets inflation, the erosion of purchasing power is largely contained in the short term. In practice, this means cash can preserve its real value better than it appears at first glance. Trying to earn significantly more than that usually changes the nature of the decision. It is no longer just about preserving capital, but about taking currency risk and moving into investment territory. The next two chapters explore that distinction in more detail.

# CHAPTER 6 :

## How to Value a Currency

*F*or most of modern history, money was not entirely abstract. It was anchored to something physical: gold. For centuries, the idea was simple: money had value because it could be exchanged for a fixed amount of a real asset. Governments guaranteed that each unit of currency could, in principle, be exchanged for a specific amount of gold at any time.

That system became formalized in the 19th century. In 1821, the United Kingdom—then the world's leading economic power after the Industrial Revolution—officially adopted the gold standard. Over time, other countries followed. Portugal (1854) and Germany (1873). France, Italy, Switzerland, Belgium, and Greece through the Latin Monetary Union in 1878. Denmark, Norway, and Sweden under the Scandinavian Monetary Union in 1875. Later on, a wide range of major economies joined the system, including Spain, Argentina, Egypt, Austria-Hungary, Russia, Japan, India, the United States[9] in 1900, and Mexico in 1904.

At its peak, the gold standard created a unified global monetary architecture. Different currencies still existed, but they were all defined by the same reference point. And because of this shared reference, currencies could be compared to one another simply by measuring how much gold each one represented (see Appendix for a practical example). Gold changed everything. Once money is tied to a fixed asset, it is no longer fully flexible. Governments could only issue currency if they held enough gold to back it. In theory, this created discipline.

Money could not expand without constraint.

To understand how the system worked, it helps to simplify it. A central bank balance sheet can be represented as follows:

*The figures are given for explanatory purposes.*

| ASSETS | LIABILITIES |
|---|---|
| GOLD 100 | MONEY IN CIRCULATION 100 |
| OTHER ASSETS[10] 100 | OTHER LIABILITIES[11] 100 |

In this framework, every unit of currency corresponds to an amount of gold. This created trust—but only as long as convertibility is credible. And history shows that this credibility was strongest in normal times, but fragile under stress.

Sometimes gold reserves were reduced. Sometimes money supply increased beyond reserves. In both cases, the result was the same: a devaluation of currency relative to gold.

Adjustments to gold parity were relatively common, especially following wars or major economic crises. These devaluations reduced the value of existing money, since each unit of currency suddenly represented a smaller amount of gold than before. The United Kingdom did this during the First World War —like most of the countries involved in the conflict. The United States did it after the Great Depression. Each time, the system bent under pressure.

To go further:

Detailed explanation on what happened, for example, in the United Kingdom during the First World War (1914–1918), and later in the United States following the Great Depression.

- The United Kingdom, like many other countries, temporarily abandoned the gold standard in order to finance the war through money issuance (via banknotes and loans) and to avoid a shortage of precious metal, much of which had been allocated to fund the war effort.

After the war, the pound sterling was no longer directly convertible into gold for some time. It was at the request of the British government in 1925, under the leadership of Winston Churchill, then Chancellor of the Exchequer[12], that the country decided to return to the gold standard at the pre-war parity. The parity, now too high (overvalued) relative to the state of the postwar British economy (marked by high debt, a depressed economy, high unemployment, and a lack of gold reserves), made the situation untenable. This is what forced the United Kingdom to permanently abandon the gold standard a few years later in 1931. This turning point marked the end of an era, signaling a handover to the U.S. dollar (which retained its gold parity), which was playing an increasingly important role in international transactions;

- In 1933, the United States temporarily abandoned its gold parity. Against the backdrop of an economic crisis and the Great Depression, the U.S. government led by Franklin D. Roosevelt adopted several measures to emerge from this crisis. A major change to the monetary system was enacted. The president issued a decree prohibiting U.S. citizens from holding gold; and the U.S. dollar's gold parity shifted from $20.67 (USD) per ounce[13] to $35 (USD) per ounce. This change led to a devaluation of the dollar relative to gold. At the same time, the ban on holding gold forced citizens to sell it to the federal government, thereby increasing U.S. gold reserves, which further solidified the new exchange rate.

The same pattern would be repeated, this time permanently, in 1971.

By the mid-20th century, the system had reached its limits. The United States, which stood at the centre of the global monetary order, began issuing more dollars than it could fully support with gold reserves.

In 1971, President Richard Nixon suspended the convertibility of the US dollar into gold. This marked the end of the gold standard. Once the United States had definitively abandoned any peg to gold, other countries gradually followed. Within a few years, the link between money and precious metals had completely disappeared. A monetary system that had lasted for nearly two centuries came to an end.

But when money is no longer tied to a fixed amount of physical assets, a new question arises: what actually gives modern currency its value?

In today's fiat monetary system, central bank gold reserves are no longer required to fully back the money in circulation, and there is no expectation that they should. Central banks may still hold gold, but it is no longer essential. Instead, we now live under a fiat system: money is backed not by gold, but by trust (from the Latin *fiducia*), and more precisely by the balance sheets of central banks and governments.

We can present a simplified version of a central bank's balance sheet as follows:

| ASSETS | LIABILITIES |
| --- | --- |
| ASSETS PORTFOLIO<br>*including gold, government bonds, and cash*<br>100 | MONEY IN CIRCULATION<br>100 |
| OTHER ASSETS[14]<br>100 | OTHER LIABILITIES[15]<br>100 |

*A detailed illustration is provided in the Appendix, showing the data for the balance sheets of the American, European, Japanese, Swiss, and Australian central banks.*

In this system, money is no longer a claim on gold. It is a claim—indirectly—on financial assets held by central banks, most importantly government bonds.

In practice, central banks often hold government debt issued by their own state. This creates a circular system: governments issue debt; central banks hold that debt; money is issued against it.

As long as governments are perceived as solvent and central banks remain credible, the system functions smoothly. But if confidence in those assets declines, the value of money can weaken as well. Because the foundation is no longer a single asset like gold. It is confidence in institutions.

## What it implies for investors

Holding money is not a neutral position. Earning income and keeping it in cash is, in effect, an indirect exposure to the assets held by the central bank.

In other words, holding cash is itself an investment decision, even if it does not feel like one. You are implicitly choosing one store of value over many others. From this perspective, currency is simply another asset. It competes with other assets to preserve your money.

This becomes even clearer when we consider how the system behaves under stress.

If government bonds lose value—for example, because public debt becomes too high and doubts emerge about the state's ability to repay—then the currency, which is closely linked to those bonds, tends to weaken as well.

Conversely, even if the composition of these assets remains stable, an expansion of the money supply still reduces the value of each unit of currency. This typically occurs during periods of war, when public spending increases sharply, during economic crises that require large-scale fiscal support, or during financial crises when governments intervene to stabilize the banking system.

The result is inflation: more units of money chasing the same amount of goods and services. These dynamics are not theoretical. They are recurring patterns that deserve attention from anyone holding currency over time.

The broader lesson is simple. No monetary system—no matter how advanced or well designed—is fully protected from extreme events such as crises or prolonged wars. Beneath the appearance of stability, every system eventually reveals its limits under sufficient stress. Understanding this is essential. It allows investors to recognize the early signs of currency weakness and to think more clearly about how to position themselves when monetary conditions begin to shift.

In most of the world today, exchange rates operate under a floating regime. By looking at a central bank's balance sheet, it is possible to estimate how many assets—such as government bonds, foreign reserves, and gold—stand behind each unit of currency in circulation. This can be thought of as a coverage ratio: the amount of underlying "real backing" per unit of money. This does not mean that currency is directly guaranteed or redeemable. It is not. But it offers a useful way to think about the structural strength of a currency. A detailed comparison of major currencies is provided in the appendix for those who wish to explore this framework further.

Other factors also influence exchange rates, such as interest rates, inflation differentials, trade and capital flows, as well as the international reach of a currency. **More fundamentally, all these factors converge on a single variable: confidence. And confidence rests on concrete foundations — primarily the government's capacity to service its debt, and the central bank's credibility in maintaining monetary stability.**

# CHAPTER 7:

## The foreign exchange market, Forex

*W*hen it comes to investing, the goal is to generate a return. This return is generated in two ways: through the interest rate it offers and through fluctuations in its exchange rate. offers and through fluctuations in its exchange rate.

It is possible to find a currency with interest rates significantly above the global average, and this can appear very attractive. But this is not sufficient on its own. The currency must also maintain its value on foreign exchange markets; otherwise, gains from interest can be offset—or even erased—by depreciation.

The case of Turkey (detailed in the Appendix) between 2002 and 2013 is often cited as a textbook example. During this period, interest rates on the Turkish lira (TRY) were very high[16] and, for a time, exceeded inflation[17]. These yields attracted substantial capital inflows, including from foreign investors. As a result, the currency remained relatively stable against major currencies, including the US dollar (USD), between 2002 and 2010.

The situation began to change when interest rates came under political pressure and started to decline. Inflation gradually caught up with nominal returns, and by the end of 2013, real interest rates had fallen close to zero. At that point, the attractiveness of the Turkish lira diminished, and capital flows began to reverse. Because the underlying strength of the central bank's balance sheet was not sufficient to reassure markets at the time (a declining coverage ratio), the currency started to depreciate around 2010. The decline was initially gradual, but it accelerated significantly over time, eventually leading to a severe long-term devaluation. In retrospect, investors exposed to the currency over the long run would have lost both principal and interest. The Turkish case illustrates a key point: a high interest rate is not a guarantee of strength. In some cases, it can temporarily support a fragile currency by compensating for weaknesses in the central bank's balance sheet. But this balance is unstable, and it tends to unravel when investor confidence shifts and capital begins to leave.

The second component of currency return—exchange rate appreciation—also has structural limits. A currency is not only a store of value and a unit of account; it is also a medium of exchange, both domestically[18] and internationally. Because all major currencies are connected through global foreign exchange markets, exchange rates cannot move in one direction indefinitely without consequences. A sustained appreciation typically weakens export competitiveness and affects the trade balance, which often leads central banks to intervene to limit further gains.

As a result, even currencies perceived as fundamentally strong cannot rise indefinitely, especially in a world where monetary policies are broadly synchronized and balance sheet quality tends to deteriorate simultaneously due to rising public debt and sovereign risk concerns. If the global economy were divided into fully isolated currency blocs, exchange rates could diverge much more dramatically. But in today's interconnected system, this is not the case. For this reason, relying on long-term exchange rate appreciation as a primary driver of wealth creation is inherently limited. It is difficult to build sustained returns from currency exposure alone. This reinforces the need to consider other asset classes for long-term capital growth.

To illustrate, the Israeli shekel (ILS) has been one of the stronger-performing currencies over the past two decades. With relatively stable interest rate differentials, it has appreciated by nearly 40% against the US dollar over that period. In early 2005, one US dollar was worth about 4.40 shekels; twenty years later, it was closer to 3.20 shekels. However, this still represents an average appreciation of less than 2% per year.

**In simple terms, a "strong" currency is one that does not show early signs of structural depreciation against major peers and offers a real (after-tax) interest rate above inflation. Such a currency can serve as a reasonable tool for capital preservation. Similar results can also come from long-term structural appreciation, although this is rare and typically limited in magnitude. By contrast, unusually high interest rates should always be interpreted with caution. They often signal underlying risks and may mask structural weaknesses in the currency itself.**

# PART III

## Real estate: A lifetime investment

# CHAPTER 8 :

## Buy or rent: the honest calculation

Once emergency savings are in place, most people face the next major decision: where to live, and whether buying a home makes more financial sense than renting. It is one of the most consequential financial choices a household will make, and also one of the most emotionally charged. That combination makes it especially prone to poor reasoning. This chapter does not tell you whether to buy or rent. Instead, it provides a framework to evaluate the decision using your own numbers, and without the emotional bias that so often distorts it.

Owning a primary residence has one argument that stands above all others: once the mortgage is fully repaid, housing costs effectively disappear. At retirement—when income typically declines—this becomes particularly significant. A paid-off home is not just an asset; it is a permanent reduction in monthly expenses. There is also a behavioral dimension. A mortgage acts as a form of forced savings. Each monthly payment builds equity over time. Renters do not benefit from this mechanism. In their case, any savings must come from deliberate discipline: the difference between rent and income has to be actively saved or invested. For most people, that discipline is inconsistent. **In the absence of strong financial habits, buying a home often leads to better outcomes simply because it removes the option not to save.**

A mortgage, in that sense, is not just a loan. It is a structured savings mechanism with legal consequences for non-payment—precisely what makes it effective for individuals who struggle to save consistently on their own.

However, renting can outperform buying under the right conditions. The logic is relatively simple. A renter who pays less each month than a homeowner's mortgage payment generates a monthly surplus. If they also avoid committing capital to a down payment, that money remains available for investment elsewhere.

If both the monthly surplus and the initial capital are consistently invested at a return higher than the property's appreciation rate[19], renting can generate greater wealth over time. If you do not buy, that capital can be deployed into alternative investments instead. The key word is consistency. This approach only works if the difference between renting and owning is invested every month, without interruption, over a long period of time. That level of discipline is rare. Over fifteen or twenty years, most households fail to maintain it. As a result, the theoretical advantage of renting often does not translate into real-world outcomes.

Ultimately, the comparison between buying and renting comes down to a simple question: which path creates more net wealth over a given time horizon? To answer it properly, you need a few key inputs (in **bold**). The table below provides a framework to estimate your net worth under both scenarios at the end of a defined period.

| PURCHASE | RENT |
|---|---|
| **Purchase price of the property** (1) | **Monthly rent** (9) |
| + | + |
| Additional costs associated with the purchase | **Average monthly expenses** (10) |
| = Cost of acquiring the dwelling (2) | |
| **Personal contribution** (3) | Personal contribution = Amount of initial investment |
| Amount borrowed (= (2) - (3)) | |
| >> | >> |
| Monthly mortgage[20] (4) | Monthly available savings for investment<br>(money saved each month because rent is lower than ownership costs)<br>(11) = (4) + (5) - (9) - (10) |
| + | |
| **Average other monthly expenses** (5) | |
| Total monthly housing cost = (4) + (5) | |

| Net worth at the end of the mortgage term | Net worth at the end of the mortgage term |
|---|---|
| = (1) x (1 + annual real estate growth rate)^ number of years | = Personal contribution x (1 + annual investment return)^ number of years<br>+<br>(11) x 12 months x (1 + annual investment return)^ 1<br>+<br>(11) x 12 x (1 + annual investment return)^ 2<br>+<br>(11) x 12 x (1 + annual investment return)^ 3<br>+<br>....<br>+<br>(11) x 12 x (1 + annual investment return)^ number of years |

With this framework, we can build a concrete example. Imagine a $300,000 property purchased with a $50,000 down payment, financed at a 5% mortgage rate, with 5% annual real estate appreciation and a 5% annual investment return. Under these assumptions, the homeowner results in approximately $1,015,000 after 25 years. By contrast, the renter invests the monthly surplus—$637 per month, defined as the difference between the mortgage payment and a $1,000 rent—at a 5% return. Over the same period, this results in approximately $517,000.

Now change just one variable: reduce real estate appreciation to 1%, while keeping everything else constant. The homeowner's outcome falls to roughly $385,000 after 25 years, while the renter's result remains unchanged at $517,000. Same inputs. Different assumption. Completely different conclusion.

Ultimately, the outcome of this comparison depends on two key variables. The first is the price-to-rent ratio in your local market—how expensive it is to buy relative to renting an equivalent property. The lower this ratio, the stronger the case for buying. The higher it is, the more attractive renting becomes, provided the savings differential is actually invested. The second is the return on the alternative investment, whether that is real estate (residential, commercial, or otherwise) or financial assets such as stocks and bonds.

**When buying is relatively inexpensive and renting is costly, monthly mortgage payments tend to be close to rent levels. In that case, renting is unlikely to outperform buying over the long term—unless the alternative investments perform exceptionally well, or the real estate market under-**

**performs expectations. Conversely, when renting is relatively inexpensive (a low price-to-rent ratio), or when one chooses a lower-cost property, monthly rent may be significantly below the cost of ownership. In such cases, renting can outperform buying—provided the difference is consistently invested and the alternative portfolio compounds at a higher rate than real estate appreciation.** The exact threshold at which one strategy overtakes the other depends on the underlying inputs, which can be modeled using a personal spreadsheet based on individual circumstances.

As a rough benchmark, using US data, when real estate appreciates at around 5% per year, buying a primary residence has often outperformed renting even against an alternative portfolio returning 8% annually. At 3% appreciation, however, the conclusion becomes less stable. Buying can win a 7%—even 8%—alternative investment under favorable conditions: a meaningful discount to market value, low financing costs, or a structure that allows a large share of capital to remain invested elsewhere. Between these scenarios lies a gray area. The tipping point depends heavily on timing, financing conditions, and the size of the down payment. The 7—8% return assumption is used here as a benchmark, as it broadly reflects the historical average performance of a 60/40 portfolio (60% equities, 40% bonds) since the 1990s[21].

Local and national factors therefore matter significantly. The results are neither universal nor static. They depend on time and place. That said, a primary residence remains a powerful long-term financial instrument, particularly when acquired under favorable conditions—something that is often achievable with sufficient planning, especially given that this is typically a long-term, low-frequency decision. Real estate also benefits from leverage and low borrowing costs when interest rates are favorable. By contrast, the alternative strategy requires sustained discipline: the entire monthly surplus must be reinvested without interruption over decades. This is a demanding constraint, and not one that most households consistently meet.

For this reason, buying a primary residence is often the right behavioral decision, even when it is not strictly the optimal financial one. It enforces a form of forced savings and creates a structural safeguard against under-investment. Finally, note that this analysis excludes capital gains taxation[22] on property and investment returns, income taxes on dividends, as well as one-off costs such as major renovations or portfolio management fees. These variables should be adjusted based on individual tax circumstances before drawing firm conclusions.

# CHAPTER 9:

## The hidden costs of real estate

*B*uying real estate, in simple terms, means purchasing land, a house, or an apartment. Beyond the right to live in it or control it, real estate also offers something else: the ability to generate income through rent. It is, by far, the largest asset class in the world across all regions and economies. If we step back and look at its long-term performance, combining both capital appreciation and rental income, real estate has historically delivered returns of around 10% per year on a gross basis over very long horizons.

In the United States, this estimate is broadly consistent with research by Favilukis, Ludvigson, and Van Nieuwerburgh[23], based on data from the 1950s to the 1970s, which places long-term annual returns in the 9% to 11% range. Once adjusted for inflation and ongoing costs such as maintenance, this translates into a real net return of roughly 5% to 7%. A similar picture emerges from the work of Jordà, Knoll, Kuvshinov, Schularick, and Taylor[24], who analyze a wide set of developed economies over an even longer period starting in 1870. For France, for example, their estimates point to an average real return of around 6% per year over more than a century.

Taken together, these studies suggest a simple conclusion: real estate has historically been a strong long-term compounder. Not because it is smooth or predictable, but because it benefits from structural forces that, over time, tend to support its value. But it is also a very specific type of asset. And two features clearly set it apart from most financial investments. The first is the presence of high entry costs at the moment of acquisition. The second is leverage: real estate is rarely purchased in full upfront, but instead financed through debt, which changes both the risk and the return profile in a fundamental way.

## The costs associated with the acquisition

Regardless of the type of investment vehicle you choose, costs are almost unavoidable. They can take the form of brokerage fees when buying financial securities, or foreign exchange commissions when converting one currency into another on the FX market. The same is true for real estate—except that in this case, the costs are often significantly higher in relative terms. Given the size of the amounts involved, they become a central variable that must be anticipated. They are numerous, material, and arise at multiple stages of the investment process.

In real estate, for example, brokerage or agency fees typically range from 1% to 6% of the property price, depending on the country— verify local rates before calculating. These fees can sometimes be avoided if you purchase directly, but in most cases they compensate professionals—real estate agents or brokers—who connect buyers and sellers, manage listings, organize viewings, assist with price negotiation, and ultimately help bring the transaction to completion. On top of that, there are legal costs linked to verifying ownership (the title deed), checking for any encumbrances such as easements or mortgages, and drafting the sale contract. Whether handled by a notary or an attorney, the contract must meet legal requirements to ensure the transaction is valid, enforceable, and binding between both parties. There are also administrative costs in the form of registration fees, which formalize ownership and make it enforceable against third parties. In other words, they ensure that your property rights cannot be challenged. Finally, there are transfer taxes and related duties that apply when ownership changes hands. They depend on the country and jurisdiction. Note that because real estate is both immobile and highly visible, it is also more exposed to taxation when governments need additional fiscal revenue.

With total transaction costs of 10%, a $300,000 property purchase means only $270,000 is actually invested in the asset. The other $30,000 is absorbed by transaction costs the moment the deal is done. So even though you spend $300,000, only $270,000 is really working for you.

Unless you work in the industry, these costs—and the complexity they imply—make real estate something you transact in infrequently. It takes time to recover them, which naturally pushes real estate toward a long-term investment horizon. The exception is when a property can be acquired below market value, allowing transaction costs to be offset and potentially creating the opportunity for a relatively short-term profit.

## Frequent recourse to borrowing

Because home purchases involve large sums of money, buying a property—often the biggest financial decision in a person's life—usually requires external financing. Most buyers do not bridge the gap between their savings and the purchase price alone. They rely either on family support or, more commonly, on a bank loan.

Getting a mortgage is a process. It often starts with opening a bank account, sometimes with associated fees. It also includes various costs such as guarantees, mortgage registration, and other lending-related charges. Once approved, the bank provides the funds on your behalf. In return, you agree to repay the loan over time, in monthly installments, with interest. That interest is expressed through the annual percentage rate (APR). It represents the bank's price for lending you money. For the borrower, this is the cost of credit: the total interest paid over the life of the loan, calculated on the remaining balance. One important feature of most mortgages is flexibility. At any point, the borrower can repay part or all of the loan early—often when selling the property. When that happens, interest payments stop immediately.

Returning to our earlier example of a $300,000 property, financing alone can cost around $80,000 over 10 years[25] at a 5% interest rate, and roughly $175,000 over 20 years[26]. Over time, the impact becomes significant. What initially looks like $270,000 effectively invested can turn into a total cost of ownership of about $380,000[27] in the first case, and around $475,000[28] in the second.

This is why real estate is so sensitive to interest rates. Small changes in rates have large effects on affordability. When rates fall, borrowing capacity increases and prices tend to rise. When rates rise, the opposite happens.

For example, with a $1,000 monthly payment, a buyer can borrow roughly $150,000[29] over 20 years at a 5% interest rate. At 3%, the same payment allows borrowing closer to $180,000[30]. In other words, interest rates don't just affect borrowing costs. They directly determine how much housing you can afford with the same monthly budget.

This last point matters because real estate often acts as a strong long-term hedge against inflation. But in the short run, high interest rates can weigh heavily on property values.

This tension becomes especially visible during episodes of hyperinflation, when the mechanism is pushed to its extreme. In such environments, inflation rises so fast that lending effectively breaks down. Loan repayments quickly lose value in real terms, making it unattractive for banks to lend money at all. As a result, interest rates become extremely high—or stop making sense altogether—and credit markets freeze. Real estate demand, which depends heavily on financing, collapses. Prices may still rise in nominal terms during these periods, but that can be misleading. Once adjusted for inflation, returns are often much weaker—and in some cases deeply negative. In the end, real estate only tends to recover once inflation stabilizes and credit markets begin to function normally again.

# CHAPTER 10 :

## Compare two real estate projects

*O*nce you have purchased a property, you can decide how to use it. One option is to rent it out. In that case, the property generates cash flow that goes directly to you. On top of any long-term appreciation, it also provides a steady stream of income over time.

To assess the profitability of a real estate investment—or any investment, for that matter—you need to think in terms of cash flows over time. Money goes out, and money comes in. Outflows include the down payment, taxes, loan repayments, maintenance costs, and any renovations. Inflows come from rent and, eventually, the resale price. The key is to organize all of this on a timeline, year by year, over the full life of the investment.

In year zero, you record the initial outflow. This includes your down payment, the purchase price if buying in cash, agent fees, legal and administrative costs, and any immediate renovation expenses.

In year 1, you will have your first income (rent), as well as your first expenses (taxes on rent, loan repayment, maintenance costs, renovations);

.

.

.

And so on until the date of the sale. This will include your income (rent and sale price this time), as well as your expenses (taxes on rental income, any capital gains tax, loan repayments, and prorated maintenance and expenses). It looks like this:

| Year 0 | Year 1 | Year 2 | ... | Final year |
|---|---|---|---|---|
| Cash-Flow 0 | Cash-Flow 1 | Cash-Flow 2 | ... | Final Cash-Flow |

Once all the data is in place, we can calculate what is known as the internal rate of return, or IRR. In simple terms, it is the rate that makes the present value of all future cash flows equal to zero.

The structure is usually the same. Year zero is negative, reflecting the initial investment. The final year is positive, driven by the resale price net of costs. In between, cash flows vary depending on the structure of the deal: the holding period, financing conditions, interest rate, and repayment schedule. In real estate, income comes from rent. But this income is never pure. It is reduced by a long list of expenses: property taxes, insurance, condominium fees, maintenance of shared spaces, management fees, repairs, and unexpected costs. If debt is involved, loan repayments must also be included.

Because of this complexity, IRR is rarely calculated by hand. It is usually computed using a spreadsheet or financial calculator, where cash flows are entered year by year and the result is generated automatically. **The investment with the highest IRR is, in theory, the most attractive.** But IRR is only as good as its assumptions. It depends heavily on the inputs used, especially the final value of the property. And that final number is the most uncertain part of the entire model. Everything else is relatively predictable. The resale price is not.

In markets with a long history of strong demand—such as major cities, university towns, tourist destinations, or established rental hubs—it is often reasonable to assume that demand will persist. In those cases, investing is less about prediction and more about continuity. Elsewhere, it becomes a bet on change. And when the goal is resale, the key question is simple: how likely is it that someone will want to buy this property in the future?

That is why location matters so much. Not just in a broad sense, but in very specific terms: proximity to jobs, transport, schools, cultural life, and everyday convenience. Quality of life matters too—quiet streets, well-maintained buildings, and a sense of order all tend to support long-term value. So does social perception: prestige, reputation, and the type of residents an area attracts. When these factors are missing, appreciation can still happen—but it usually depends on transformation. Sometimes planned, through infrastructure, transport, or redevelopment. Sometimes organic, through gradual gentrification as higher-income households move in and reshape demand. In both cases, prices follow people.

IRR is also a useful way to compare different real estate strategies. It allows you to evaluate choices that look very different on the surface: buying in one city versus another, flipping immediately, renovating and then selling, renovating while renting before selling, long-term rental, or simply holding a property indefinitely.

**In practice, the most effective real estate strategy often follows a simple pattern. Find an undervalued asset. Buy it below market price. Improve it through renovation. Generate income through rent while holding it. Then sell it at the right moment. Repeated over time, this cycle can produce strong results, and few approaches outperform it when executed well.**

**IRR is also a useful way to test variations of the same project by adjusting key assumptions, especially the initial investment. This makes it possible to see how returns change under different capital allocations and to identify where the strategy becomes most efficient.**

# PART IV

## Bonds: A misunderstood asset class

# CHAPTER 11 :

## What are bonds, and why do most investors undervalue them?

Once you have set aside your emergency fund, which simply sits there waiting, you can move forward with more clarity. The rest of your capital now has a purpose. If you have a meaningful project ahead—buying a home or a rental property, financing education, moving abroad, changing careers, starting or acquiring a business, renovating your home, or making a planned large purchase such as a car—you are usually working toward a known time horizon. The timing may not be exact, but it is rarely infinite. This creates a specific problem: where do you park that money in the meantime?

You need something that is safe, liquid, and still able to earn a return while you wait. Bonds are one of the few assets that tend to meet these three conditions.

Over short horizons, cash earns very little. Real estate is inefficient due to high transaction costs. Commodities like gold preserve value over long periods but do not generate income. Equities, on the other hand, are often too volatile when the time horizon is short. This is where the mismatch becomes dangerous.

Imagine investing in stocks just before a 9- to 18-month market downturn—something that is entirely normal in equity cycles. Once that happens, you are left with an uncomfortable choice: sell at a loss, or delay your project and wait for recovery, with no clear timeline.

**This is why bonds tend to fit better when the goal is**

**defined and the horizon is limited, typically in the 2- to 5-year range.** Even outside of specific projects, they can still play a stabilizing role in a broader portfolio. But like any asset class, their role depends on their characteristics, risks, and what kind of return they can realistically be expected to deliver.

But what exactly is a bond? A bond is, at its core, a loan. When you buy one, you are lending money to an issuer—usually a government or a company. In return, you receive a written promise: they will pay you interest, and repay the principal at a fixed date. That interest is the price of trust. It compensates you for the risk that something goes wrong: default, delays, or the costs of recovery through legal and administrative processes.

In simple terms, a bond is a contract. You lend $1,000 today. In return, you receive regular interest payments along the way, and your $1,000 back at maturity—whether that is in 2, 5, or 10 years.

One important feature of bonds is that time is built into the contract. And time matters. In normal conditions, the longer you agree to lend your money, the higher the interest rate you receive. This relationship is known as the yield curve. At its simplest, the yield curve reflects a trade-off not so much between risk levels, but between time horizons. Bank deposits work in a similar way. When you deposit money in a bank, you are also lending it—just in a more flexible form. You expect to get it back on demand. Because deposits sit at the center of the financial system, they are often partially protected by public authorities[31]. In practice, this makes them feel very safe.

But in practice, you could bypass the bank and lend directly to the government instead. Is that riskier? Not necessarily. In many cases, sovereign debt can be as safe—or even safer—than the banking system[32] that distributes it.

Yet there is a difference in return. Short-term bank rates are usually lower than what you can earn by lending to the government over longer periods. That difference is the yield curve in action. The trade-off, again, is not mainly risk. It is time.

But that only holds if you can stay invested until maturity. If you need to exit early—because of a financial shock or simply a change of plans—you may not get the return you expected. Bonds are traded on markets, and their prices move up and down. Selling before maturity introduces market risk, and losses are possible.

The risk, then, does not come from the bond itself. It comes from a mismatch between the investment and the investor's needs. Most mistakes are not caused by choosing the wrong asset, but by choosing the wrong time horizon.

This is why an emergency fund comes first. **Once short-term needs are covered, the rest of your capital can be invested with a longer perspective.** The further away the money is from being needed, the more flexibility you have in seeking higher returns.

In some countries, this process is reinforced by the structure of the financial system itself. In France, for example, regulated savings accounts[33] are subject to strict limits. Once those limits are reached, investors who want to put additional savings to work must look elsewhere.

One simple way to maintain flexibility is to spread investments across different maturities. Instead of committing everything for the same length of time, capital is distributed along a range of horizons. This creates options. Some funds become available sooner, reducing the risk of being forced to sell an investment at an unfavorable moment simply because cash is needed.

At its core, investing is always a balance between risk, return, and time. Expected return can be thought of as the probability of an outcome multiplied by the value of that outcome. The goal is not simply to maximize returns, but to maximize them within the constraints of your own timeline.

**Once the investment horizon extends beyond a year or two, bonds become a credible alternative to cash.** But this naturally leads to another question: within the bond universe itself, which investments offer the most attractive balance between risk and return?

# CHAPTER 12 :

## How to calculate bond yields

*E*very borrower has a certain level of financial stability. For individuals, this is reflected in a credit score in the United States, as well as in many other countries. For organizations—such as corporations, municipalities, and sovereign states—this creditworthiness is expressed through a rating. This is the core business of credit rating agencies.

Assessing that creditworthiness is the role of credit rating agencies. Their job is to evaluate how likely a borrower is to repay its obligations in full and on time. To do so, they analyze a wide range of factors: financial statements, cash flow generation, debt levels, management quality, and repayment history. Based on this analysis, they assign a rating that summarizes the borrower's perceived financial strength. These ratings provide investors with a common language for comparing risk across thousands of issuers. The methodology behind them has been developed over decades and is widely used throughout global financial markets. That said, ratings are not predictions, nor are they infallible. They are informed opinions based on the information available at a given point in time. Financial conditions can change, management teams can make mistakes, and unexpected events can alter a borrower's ability to repay.

Today, the global credit rating industry is dominated by three private agencies: S&P Global, Moody's, and Fitch Ratings. Together, they provide the ratings that serve as a benchmark for much of the world's bond market. The table below shows the rating scales used by the major agencies and the correspondence between them.

| S&P / Fitch | Moody's | Credit Risk | Category |
|---|---|---|---|
| AAA | Aaa | Exceptional | Investment |
| AA | Aa | Excellent | |
| A | A | Solid | |
| BBB | Baa | Average[34] | |
| BB | Ba | Speculative | Speculative[35] |
| B | B | Highly Speculative | |
| CCC | Caa | High risk | |
| CC / C | Ca | Very close to the default | |
| D / SD | C | In default of payment | Default |

Each rating is associated with a credit risk (default). This is the risk that an unforeseen negative event will occur during the loan period. This event can be:

- a delay or failure to pay interest, principal (amount loaned), or even both simultaneously;
- bankruptcy or judicial receivership preventing timely payment of interest and/or principal;
- a debt restructuring or an imposed debt exchange that is unfavorable to creditors (distressed exchanges).

To estimate the risk associated with each credit rating, investors often look at historical default data. Credit rating agencies publish extensive statistics showing how frequently borrowers in each rating category have failed to meet their obligations over time. These figures are based on past experience, which means they vary depending on the period studied and the sample observed. As a result, there is no single universal default rate. Instead, each rating category is associated with a range of outcomes that reflects how similar borrowers have performed in the past.

At its core, bond investing is a simple trade-off. The higher the probability of default, the higher the return investors demand in exchange. Risk and return are inseparable. This relationship is intuitive as in these cases, investors are not relying on personal trust or familiarity. They are lending to organizations they may never meet, based solely on publicly available information. The return they receive compensates them not only for the possibility of losing money, but also for uncertainty itself.

And default is rarely a clean event. When a borrower stops making payments, recovering capital can become a long and frustrating process. Legal procedures, negotiations, court filings, and administrative costs all consume time and resources. In practice, investors often discover that a default is not a single event but a process. The process usually begins when the issuer can no longer meet its interest or principal payments. From there, two outcomes are common: restructuring or bankruptcy.

In a restructuring, the borrower and its creditors negotiate new terms. Repayment may be delayed, interest payments reduced, existing bonds exchanged for new ones, or debt partially converted into equity.

Bankruptcy is more severe. Assets are sold, and the proceeds are distributed according to a legal order of priority. Bondholders often recover only part of their investment, and sometimes very little

Meanwhile, the bond itself may trade at a steep discount in the secondary market. Investors who choose—or are forced—to sell during this period often do so at a significant loss. This is why higher-risk borrowers must offer higher yields. Investors need compensation not only for the probability of default, but also for the uncertainty and potential losses that accompany it.

<u>To understand the vocabulary:</u>

In finance, the return offered by a bond is commonly referred to as its yield. A bond's yield can be viewed as the sum of two components. The first is the risk-free rate—the return available on the safest securities in the market. The second is the credit spread: the additional return investors require for accepting the borrower's specific risk.

In other words: yield = risk-free rate + spread

with

- risk-free rate: generally the interest rate of short-term bonds in the country concerned (3 months, 6 months or 1 year); or 10 years, depending on the duration of the investment envisaged;
- the "spread", corresponding to the additional risk premium you require to compensate for the risk of default.

# CHAPTER 13 :

## Credit ratings and the risk/return trade-off

Below is the average cumulative probability of default over a ten (10) year period. It includes data collected by the rating agency Moody's based on the 1999 Moody's report published by Keenan, Shtogrin, and Sobenhart; data from the February 2009 Moody's Global Credit Policy report for the reference period 1920-2008; and then for the periods 1970-2008, 1983-2008, and 1998-2008.

| S&P / Fitch | Moody's | Report Moody's - 1999 | 1920 - 2008 | 1970 - 2008 | 1983 - 2008 | 1998 - 2008 |
|---|---|---|---|---|---|---|
| AAA | Aaa | 0.77% | 0.86% | 0.51% | 0.19% | 0.04% |
| AA | Aa | 0,99% | 2.27% | 0.55% | 0.41% | 0.00% |
| A | A | 1.55% | 3.13% | 1.75% | 1.71% | 3.85% |
| BBB | Yes | 4.39% | 7.02% | 4.40% | 4.14% | 2.34% |
| BB | Not | 20.63% | 18.44% | 18.28% | 18.74% | 11.37% |
| B | B | 43.91% | 34.29% | 41.09% | 41.45% | 34.99% |
| CCC | Caa | N/A | N/A | N/A | 64.78% | 45.13% |
| CC / C | As/C | N/A | N/A | N/A | 74.99% | N/A |

Regarding the risk premium, the average spreads observed are shown below[36], for bonds at maturity ten (10) years, per risk category:

- 0.63, for a historical average spread between +0.4% and +0.80% per year in AAA category;
- 0.91, for a historical average spread between +0.7% and +1.0% in AA category;
- 1.21, for a historical average spread between +1.0% and +1.3% in category A;
- 1.78, for a historical average spread between +1.5% and +2.0% in BBB category;
- 3.08, for a historical average spread between +2.5% and +3.5% in category BB;
- 5.08, for an average historical spread between +4.0% and +6.0% in category B;
- 9.78, for a historical average spread of +6% and more in CCC categories, and more below.

These spreads should be viewed as averages rather than fixed values. In reality, a credit spread is a market price, and like any market price, it constantly changes. It moves with interest rates, liquidity conditions, investor sentiment, and many other factors. In other words, spreads are volatile.

However, a default does not necessarily mean a total loss. In many cases, investors recover part of their capital. This is known as the recovery rate. It shows the percentage of the bond's face value that can be recovered after a default[37]. These recovery rates vary significantly across credit categories. Historically, they have tended to be higher for stronger borrowers and lower for weaker ones. Over a one-year horizon, average recovery rates have been approximately 54% for AA-rated issuers, 51% for A, 46% for BBB, 41% for BB, 34% for B, 25% for CCC, 22% for CC, and 17% for C-rated issuers.

Taking both factors into account—default probabilities and recovery rates—we can form a more realistic picture of the true economic cost of default. Assuming a risk-free rate of 3% and the average credit spreads shown above, the following table illustrates the expected outcome of a $1,000 investment over a ten-year horizon.

| S&P / Fitch | Moody's | Report Moody's - 1999 | 1920 - 2008 | 1970 - 2008 | 1983 - 2008 | 1998 - 2008 |
|---|---|---|---|---|---|---|
| AAA | Aaa | 1'358[38] | 1'358 | 1'360 | 1'362 | 1'369 |
| AA | Aa | 1'384 | 1'377 | 1'387 | 1'388 | 1'391 |
| A | A | 1'410 | 1'400 | 1'409 | 1'409 | 1'397 |
| BBB | Yes | 1'443 | 1'423 | 1'444 | 1'446 | 1'458 |
| BB | Not | 1'415 | 1'437 | 1'439 | 1'432 | 1'510 |
| B | B | 1'306 | 1'409 | 1'336 | 1'331 | 1'404 |
| CCC | Caa | N/A | N/A | N/A | 1'278 | 1'455 |
| CC / C | As/C | N/A | N/A | N/A | N/A | N/A |

What do the calculations show? They show that 10-year yields tend to increase as credit ratings decline—in other words, as default risk rises. This relationship holds consistently up to the BBB rating category. Beyond that point, the pattern becomes less stable. It is not always the case that BB-rated bonds outperform BBB-rated bonds; returns are broadly similar, and the relative winner depends on the time period used for comparison.

**In broad terms, assuming sufficient diversification—where portfolio performance tends to converge toward underlying probabilities—the BBB category appears to offer the most attractive risk-return balance over a 10-year horizon.** It sits at the lowest end of investment grade: still considered "safe" in institutional terms, but with higher yield potential than higher-rated segments. At this level, fundamentals are generally strong enough that investing is not a speculative bet on survival. It is not an exercise in hoping the issuer avoids default, nor a strategy based on finding a greater fool to sell to later. It remains firmly within the realm of investment-grade credit. **By contrast, BB-rated bonds can be more appealing in diversified, actively managed strategies, but they are less suited to a long-term buy-and-hold approach over a decade.**

BB-rated securities occupy a unique position. They offer higher yields than investment-grade bonds while maintaining relatively low average default rates—around 1% per year. However, they are also subject to structural constraints. Many institutional investors are required to sell a bond if it is downgraded from BBB to BB. This forced selling creates temporary price distortions, often pushing yields higher and generating opportunities for investors who are able to hold through the downgrade. At the same time, this segment is significantly more sensitive to credit cycles and macroeconomic conditions. As ratings decline, default rates become more volatile and increasingly tied to the broader economic environment. In lower-rated segments, the dispersion of default rates can easily double within a single year. This means that short- to medium-term volatility can be substantial, particularly for investors who do not hold to maturity. Early exits may result in capital losses, often at heavily discounted prices. In addition, as default risk increases, bond performance becomes more dependent on recovery rates. These recovery rates are difficult to estimate in advance, highly uncertain, and tend to deteriorate when economic conditions worsen.

**At the highest end of the credit spectrum, AAA-rated securities—typically issued by the most financially stable governments or institutions[39]—and AA-rated bonds—issued by very high-quality sovereigns or corporations—offer very low yields. After tax and inflation, real returns are often close to zero or even negative.** These instruments therefore function primarily as capital preservation tools rather than sources of long-term growth. A-rated bonds occupy a middle ground. In a stable inflation environment around 2%, they can deliver modest but positive real returns over time.

A key point is that credit markets are not about finding

the highest yield. At first glance, it seems intuitive that moving lower in credit quality simply means higher returns. More risk, more reward. But as you move down the credit spectrum, something counterintuitive happens: higher yields do not always translate into better outcomes. The relationship between risk and return becomes less stable, and over certain periods it can break down entirely.

This is where the nature of the trade-off begins to change. Below investment grade (BB and lower), bonds are classified as "high-yield" or "junk" bonds. In theory, their higher interest rates should compensate for higher default risk, making them more profitable overall—the gains from performing bonds offsetting losses from defaults. In practice, this is not always the case. There are three main reasons for this divergence:

- correlation during a crisis (domino effect). The problem is that low-quality bonds (junk bonds) tend to default simultaneously during a crisis. In 2008 or 2020, for example, diversification did not protect investors, and all vulnerable companies plummeted together. This is known as systemic risk;
- the "recovery rate." When an AAA government bond defaults—which is very rare—investors often recover a large portion of their principal after restructuring. This is not the case with low-quality bonds (rated B or CCC), where the recovery rate is often very low (sometimes only 20% of the initial principal). The capital loss can then completely wipe out the gains generated by interest, even when those gains are high;
- transaction costs and liquidity. AAA bonds sell in a second, while "low-quality" bonds are very difficult to sell during a panic. You will be forced to sell them at a steep discount in order to find a buyer and liquidate them quickly.

<u>To go further:</u>

Credit rating agencies assess bond quality by evaluating the same thing: the borrower's ability to repay and the probability of default at regular intervals. However, they are different companies. The methodology used to establish the rating also differs; it's their expertise. Each agency publishes default rates, transition matrices, and recovery rates for each rating. This explains why, in practice, default probabilities are not always identical for a specific category. Here they are:

| S&P | Cumulative default probabilities over 10 years[40] | Moody's | Cumulative default probabilities over 10 years |
|---|---|---|---|
| AAA | 0,67% | Aaa | 0,77% |
| AA | 0,65% | Aa | 0,99% |
| A | 1,03% | A | 1,55% |
| BBB | 2,86% | Yes | 4,39% |
| BB | 10,44% | Not | 20,63% |
| B | 22,02% | B | 43,91% |
| CCC | 50,43% | Caa | 67,52% |
| CC / C | | That | > 70% |
| D / SD | N/A | C | 100% |

We can thus see that the difference in default rates between the two rating systems becomes more pronounced as the rating gets lower. However, the correlations between the two are widely used, so that in practice, investors group bonds by rating, regardless of the issuer or the rating agency that conducted the assessment.

In practice, a BB-rated security (S&P/Fitch) and a Ba-rated security (Moody's), although in the same market classification (both belonging to the broad "high speculative grade" risk category), are not perfectly equivalent in terms of probability of default. The same applies to a B-rated security. A "Moody's B" is therefore also not equivalent to an "S&P B" in terms of actual risk.

<u>There are three reasons for this:</u>

1) Companies whose ratings are withdrawn (at the request of the bond

issuer or due to a lack of sufficient financial information allowing the rating agency to do its job properly) are removed from the panel. Defaults therefore disappear from the data even though they did in fact occur. They simply occurred while the bond was unrated at the time the panel was established. Moody's makes adjustments to reinstate them and track the issuer's rating at the time of default, thereby linking the default to its final rating. S&P Global does not make these adjustments and removes withdrawn ratings from its panel without reinstating them.

Here is a comparison of the two rating agencies when Moody's has not made the adjustment.

| S&P | Cumulative default probabilities over 10 years | Moody's | Cumulative default probabilities over 10 years - Unadjusted |
|---|---|---|---|
| AAA | 0,67% | Aaa | 0,36% |
| AA | 0,65% | Aa | 0,34% |
| A | 1,03% | A | 0,87% |
| BBB | 2,86% | Yes | 2,87% |
| BB | 10,44% | Not | 11,40% |
| B | 22,02% | B | 24,59% |
| CCC | 50,43% | Caa / C | 41,18% |
| CC / C | N/A | | |
| D / SD | N/A | | |

We then observe that when Moody's rates are calculated without adjusting for migrations and withdrawn ratings (in the same way as in the S&P Global methodology), this slightly increases the difference between the two measures of cumulative rates for high ratings; but it brings them considerably closer for low ratings.

2) Differences also exist in the definition of what constitutes a default. Moody's generally includes distressed exchanges, whereas S&P Global has historically used a slightly more restrictive definition, placing

greater emphasis on actual non-payment. Certain restructurings are treated differently;

3) Over a 10-year period, many BB/B issuers are downgraded to CCC or lower before defaulting[41]. Moody's changes ratings less frequently, meaning an issuer remains at a given rating for longer before defaulting; whereas S&P Global is slightly more reactive, with issuers often downgraded prior to default. There is therefore a mathematically higher probability that a default will occur under the new, lower rating. This is why some defaults are associated with higher ratings at Moody's.

<u>Conclusion:</u>

In summary, Moody's takes a more conservative long-term approach, although it may underestimate the likelihood of a rapid downgrade. S&P Global's ratings, on the other hand, are more dynamic and therefore prudent for stress tests designed to assess the immediate quality of the security. The firm captures downgrades more quickly, which is useful for dynamic portfolio management, particularly in the short term. However, this is less useful in the context of calculations made over the long term.

# CHAPTER 14 :

## Foreign currency bonds

The calculations were made using debt denominated in U.S. dollars. As a reminder, the risk-free rate is not universal. It depends on the currency and the country in which you invest. In the United States, the risk-free rate is typically based on U.S. government securities—short-term Treasury Bills (3-month, 6-month, or 1-year) or, more commonly in long-term analysis, 10-year Treasury Notes. In other countries, the logic is the same, but the reference changes. If a company borrows in its own currency—Turkish lira in Turkey, for example—the risk-free rate will be based on local government bonds, such as 10-year Turkish government debt. The framework is identical everywhere; only the underlying data differs. In these cases, the risk-free rate is often higher. This is not because investors earn more in real terms, but because they require compensation for currency risk—particularly the risk of devaluation driven by inflation or expected inflation.

Default probabilities also vary by region. Credit rating agencies publish historical default rates by geography and rating category, based on long-term data. For example, S&P Global[42] provides cumulative default statistics for corporate issuers across different regions over extended time periods, such as 1981 to 2020. These inputs—risk-free rates and default probabilities—are therefore not fixed constants. They are statistical estimates that depend on time, geography, and economic conditions.

| S&P / Fitch | World | United States | Europe | Emerging Markets and Frontiers |
|---|---|---|---|---|
| AAA | 0.67% | 0.81% | 0.00% | 0.00% |
| AA | 0.65% | 0.96% | 0.27% | 0.00% |
| A | 1.03% | 1.57% | 0.36% | 0.03% |
| BBB | 2.86% | 3.80% | 1.43% | 2.11% |
| BB | 10.44% | 11.92% | 6.13% | 7.00% |
| B | 22.02% | 23.16% | 16.81% | 16.52% |
| CCC / C | 50.43% | 55.07% | 34.29% | 31.04% |

# PART V

## Raw materials: A bulwark against inflation

# CHAPTER 15 :

## What influences the prices of raw materials

*W*hat should we think about "hard assets"? These are assets that exist in physical form and serve a direct, practical function in the economy. Unlike currencies or bonds, their value does not depend on an issuer—whether a government, a financial institution, or a corporation. Instead, their worth comes from their usefulness in production, consumption, or transformation.

Metals, for example, are used in industrial applications such as electronics, batteries, solar panels, and infrastructure. Energy commodities are consumed directly, whether for heating in the case of natural gas or transportation in the case of oil. Agricultural commodities are used as food, either directly or indirectly through livestock and food processing. Real estate also belongs to this category, providing shelter through use and potentially generating income through rent.

Illustration of the main categories of household spending since 1857 :

| Later[43] | 1857[44] | 1895[45] | 1960[46] - France | 1960[47] - United States | 2024[48] - France | 2024[49] - United States |
|---|---|---|---|---|---|---|
| Food | 55% | 67% | 31% | 26% | 12% | 13% |
| Clothing | 18% | 15% | 14% | 10% | 3% | 2% |
| Accommodation | 12% | 8% | 12% | 14% | 20% | 27% |
| Heating/Lighting | 5% | 6% | 4% | 6% | 5% | 6% |

We can see, therefore, that over time, spending on food has declined, as has spending on clothing. In contrast, housing costs have remained steady or increased. We also see the emergence of a new major category of spending: transportation. This category is of particular interest because a significant portion of it is directly consumed in the form of energy resources (oil). This contribution is in addition to heating and lighting expenses, which have not disappeared. However, the raw materials used have changed over time: coal, wood, or lighting gas in the past; city gas or electricity today. Let us not forget, moreover, that electricity is not produced by magic. Globally, about one-third of electricity is currently generated from coal (particularly in China and India) and one-quarter from natural gas (particularly in Europe and the United States), although other sources are growing rapidly: renewables (hydro, wind, solar); or carbon-free sources[50] (nuclear).

Since we have already discussed real estate, we can now focus more specifically on commodities. Their value is not based on a promise of payment, but on their physical reality, scarcity, and utility. This is what is known as "use value." It creates a form of independence from the financial system, since the value is embedded in the asset itself rather than in an issuer's balance sheet. In this sense, commodities can act as a store of value outside the monetary system.

But what determines their price? In simple terms, it is what market participants are willing to pay at any given moment. Commodity exchanges establish these prices by continuously matching supply and demand. When a market becomes the main reference point for pricing an asset, it is called a benchmark market.

If you want to observe or transact at what is generally considered a "fair" price, you typically refer to these benchmark exchanges. For precious metals, the reference is the London Bullion Market Association[51] (LBMA), which sets the global over-the-counter benchmark for gold and silver. For base metals such as aluminum, copper, nickel, lead, and zinc, the reference is the London Metal Exchange[52] (LME). In energy markets, Brent crude oil serves as the global benchmark for oil pricing, while West Texas Intermediate (WTI) is the key U.S. benchmark, physically delivered to Cushing[53], Oklahoma. In agriculture, the Chicago Board of Trade[54] (CBOT) sets reference prices for staples such as wheat, corn, and soybeans.

There are also more unusual benchmark markets. One example is the Aalsmeer flower auction in the Netherlands, where millions of flowers arrive each morning from countries such as Kenya, Ethiopia, Ecuador, and Colombia. Prices are set through a Dutch auction mechanism: they start high and then decline rapidly on a large clock until the first buyer presses a button. At the core of it all, prices reflect the interaction between scarcity and utility. A widely available commodity with easy production will tend to remain inexpensive, even if it is useful. A scarce resource with limited reserves or difficult extraction becomes more valuable.

**It is this combination of utility and scarcity that gives certain commodities their inflation-linked behavior.** When fiat currency loses purchasing power, commodity prices tend to rise. The underlying resource does not change, but the value of money does.

Over the very long term, however, this role is not guaranteed. Substitution matters. If a cheaper or more efficient alternative emerges, demand for the original commodity can decline. This has already happened in textiles, where polyester has replaced many natural fibers such as wool, high-quality cotton, and silk, driven by both cost advantages and functional properties like durability and ease of maintenance.

Another key factor is the breadth of usage across industries. Commodities with diversified demand tend to be more stable over time. Copper is a clear example: it is used in construction, electronics, transportation, and industrial machinery. This diversification reduces volatility, since weakness in one sector can be offset by strength in another. Because economic cycles do not move in perfect synchrony across industries, this cross-sector demand tends to make certain commodities more resilient and smoother in price behavior over time.

Unlike financial assets such as bonds or equities, commodities do not generate income[55]. They do not pay interest or dividends. They do not pay interest or dividends. Because of this, they are especially sensitive to the interest rate environment.

When interest rates are high, investors can earn a return simply by holding cash or investing in fixed income. This creates an opportunity cost for holding non-yielding assets like commodities, which tends to reduce demand and put downward pressure on prices. When rates are low, this opportunity cost declines, and commodities become relatively more attractive as stores of value.

Another important driver of commodity prices is speculation. During periods of geopolitical tension or financial stress, investors often move toward tangible assets, with gold being the most prominent example. This "safe haven" demand can push prices higher, sometimes independently of underlying supply and demand conditions.

Beyond these factors, commodities also exhibit a form of interdependence that is often overlooked. Many of them tend to move in similar directions, meaning that shocks in one segment can spill over into others. This is particularly visible in agricultural markets, especially grains. There are several reasons for this:

- The inputs are relatively similar across all grains. Production costs—including the price of farmland, fertilizer, tractors, and the fuel needed to run them—are rising simultaneously, which obviously has an impact on the selling price. Since the number of farms is immense, it is highly likely that a producer will decide to reduce their margins (for their own reasons) in order to sell their crop, putting downward pressure on their peers' prices;
- There is a phenomenon of substitutability. The nutritional value of one grain relative to another is relatively similar, and if the price of one grain rises too much compared to another, it is easy to switch. Whether for a person's own consumption or for a livestock farmer to feed their animals. A knock-on effect of rising prices generally occurs if the price of one grain increases too much. The outbreak of war between Russia and Ukraine in February 2022 demonstrates this. Because it involves two global players in the wheat sector[56], the conflict is deeply disrupting agricultural markets[57] and shaking up prices, causing global wheat prices to double in a matter of weeks, with a knock-on effect on all other substitute grains, be-

fore prices fall back in 2023, thanks to good harvests and market adjustments;

- Farmers' choices. Every year, farmers have the choice to plant whatever crop they want. If, for example, there is too much corn on the market and its price falls, the following year they will tend to want to plant something else, such as soybeans. As a result, the following year, the supply of corn will decrease and its price will rise. The supply of soybeans, on the other hand, will rise and their price will fall[58]. Conversely, when the price of corn rises sharply, farmers around the world plant it for the following year to take advantage of the price increase. This results in overproduction and a drop in prices. This seesaw effect forces prices to remain within a consistent range relative to one another.

However, they do not all behave in a completely identical way because:

- Corn is closely linked to energy. It is used in the production of fuel (ethanol). The demand for corn for food and energy therefore regularly competes. If the price of oil falls, corn prices may drop, while wheat, for example, used solely for food, remains stable.
- Soybeans are closely linked to China (which is a massive importer). They are widely used there for livestock feed (pig farms). A swine fever crisis in China will cause soybean prices to fall, but not necessarily wheat prices;
- Rice is the most self-sufficient crop. It feeds humans but is rarely used for animal feed or biofuel. Therefore, it doesn't necessarily follow the same logic as corn or soybeans. Its production is primarily dependent on the monsoons in Asia.

While grains are interchangeable with one another, they are also indirectly linked to energy markets. In particular, they compete with oil through the production of biofuels—corn-based ethanol and vegetable oil used for biodiesel. As a result, movements in hydrocarbon prices can have a direct impact on agricultural commodities.

The 2007–2008 food crisis illustrates this dynamic clearly. A sharp increase in oil prices, which reached nearly $147 per barrel, raised the cost of fertilizers, irrigation (through pumping), and transportation. These higher input costs fed directly into agricultural production, pushing grain prices higher. At the same time, rising oil prices made biofuels more economically attractive. As fuel prices increased, producing energy from crops became more profitable, redirecting part of agricultural supply away from food markets. The result was a combination of forces: lower effective food supply, steady and growing global demand—particularly in emerging economies such as China and India, where rising incomes increased meat and processed food consumption and therefore livestock feed demand—and sharply rising prices.

More broadly, fluctuations in oil prices amplify traditional drivers of agricultural markets. Weather conditions, such as the droughts in Australia and poor harvests in Europe during 2006–2007, can reduce supply. Political measures, such as export restrictions imposed by producing countries during periods of stress, can further constrain availability. And in extreme cases, geopolitical tensions or wars can directly disrupt production and trade flows.

In this sense, energy, agriculture, and geopolitics are not separate forces. They interact and reinforce each other, often turning local shocks into global price movements.

# CHAPTER 16 :

## Understanding the futures markets

Commodity markets are very often futures markets. In fact, they account for roughly 80 to 90% of total trading volume. Understanding how these markets work, and especially the distinction between "spot" and "futures" pricing, is therefore essential.

The spot price is the price of a commodity for immediate delivery. It is the price at which an asset can be exchanged right now—cash for goods. In everyday terms, it is similar to the price you pay when you buy something in a supermarket. A futures price, by contrast, is a price agreed today for delivery at a future date. It is set through a futures contract, which defines the terms of exchange between two parties at a specified point in time. This contract is a binding commitment. It can be traded multiple times before expiration, but at maturity it must be settled according to its original terms. A futures contract therefore includes:

- the seller to deliver the promised quantity of merchandise[59] on the fixed date (expiry date of the forward contract);
- the buyer to take delivery and pay the total price fixed at the time of signing the contract (regardless of whether the market price has fallen in the meantime).

Under this contract, the seller agrees to deliver the raw material at a later date, for example in six months, instead of now. Therefore, one must "pay for the time that passes."

| In other words: |
|---|
| Future price = spot price + carrying cost + expectations |

with

- The cost of carrying[60] including storage (rental of the silo or tank), insurance (against the risk of theft, damage, fire), and indirectly the opportunity cost (by buying oil to store it for example, your money is "locked up" and you do not earn the interest that this money could have earned if invested otherwise);
- And expectations. These are more “speculative” mechanisms” anticipating, or more precisely attempting to predict what supply and demand will be in the future (drought in Australia in 6 months for wheat, seasonality making natural gas almost always more expensive in winter than in summer, closure of the Strait of Hormuz in 3 months increasing the price of oil).

To secure the contract, the buyer posts a deposit known as margin, which typically represents only a small fraction of the total contract value. This is the only amount paid upfront when entering a futures position; the remaining value is settled at expiration.

Futures contracts are widely used in commodity markets because they reduce uncertainty. They allow producers to lock in future selling prices and secure a predictable income stream —whether they are mining companies, farmers, or oil producers—while buyers, typically industrial users, can secure access to raw materials at a known cost. In this way, futures markets provide visibility over future prices and allow for more stable commercial planning in both production and consumption. If a contract is held to maturity, it becomes binding. In the case of physical settlement, the exchange delivers the underlying commodity directly to the buyer—or arranges its delivery—whether via barge along the Mississippi River or into a storage facility in Dunkirk. The buyer then becomes responsible for the logistics, storage, and associated costs. Delivery specifications vary depending on the exchange and the commodity, which makes these details essential.

Although these markets are designed primarily for professional users such as farmers, producers, and industrial buyers, they carry significant risks for individuals. Because margin requirements are low relative to contract size, futures provide substantial leverage and can quickly amplify gains and losses. In some cases, contracts are cash-settled rather than physically[61] delivered. In these situations, the position is closed in monetary terms. If the settlement price is higher than the entry price, the investor makes a gain (in addition to the initial margin). If the price moves against the position, losses are deducted from the margin, and additional funds may be required if the margin is insufficient.

For these reasons, **futures markets are, in practice, designed primarily for professionals. Although they are generally accessible to individual investors, their real utility lies in the day-to-day operations of businesses.** For example, a farmer can sell part of his future harvest in advance, ensuring it will be sold at a known price at harvest time. The same logic applies to all producers of raw materials. On the other side, industrial buyers such as manufacturers secure their supply in advance, ensuring access to the inputs needed to maintain production at a predetermined cost.

**These markets also serve as powerful hedging instruments.** A farmer may hedge against the risk of a poor harvest, while an airline may hedge against rising fuel prices. The mechanism is simple. An airline can buy oil futures contracts. If oil prices rise, fuel becomes more expensive—hurting operating costs—but the futures position generates a gain that offsets the increase. If prices fall, the futures position loses value, but fuel becomes cheaper. In both cases, the overall impact tends to cancel out. This is the essence of hedging: not maximizing returns, but reducing uncertainty. The goal is stability, not speculation.

## What this means for you in the short term

Companies use futures markets to manage costs and hedge against price fluctuations. For them, these instruments are part of operations. For individual investors, however, the same markets are often reduced to something else: speculation.

Speculation in futures also comes with a structural feature that changes everything: leverage. **It is inherently risky, and it can easily lead to losses that exceed the initial capital invested.**

The reason lies in the margin system.To open a position, only a small deposit is required. This is the margin. Suppose you take exposure to $100 worth of wheat. A broker may require only $10 upfront. You now control a position ten times larger than your initial capital. This asymmetry matters. If the price falls from $100 to $80, the position loses $20. Industrial users absorb this kind of move as part of their input costs. For a pasta manufacturer, for example, whether wheat costs $80 or $100 per ton does not fundamentally alter the business model. The company needed the raw material regardless. Even if the hedge results in a loss, it has secured supply and reduced uncertainty around input costs. In that sense, the transaction serves an operational purpose rather than a purely financial one. **For a retail investor using physical settlement contracts, the situation is different. If the position is not closed, the investor may ultimately be required to take delivery of the underlying commodity, which is rarely practical. As a result, positions is typically closed before expiration, virtually any price[62].**

There is another, more structural limitation. **Futures are not designed to be long-term investment instruments. They track spot prices reasonably well in the short run, but over**

**longer horizons the relationship becomes imperfect. This makes them unsuitable for passive exposure.** Long-term holding also requires constant adjustment. Because contracts expire, positions must be rolled forward repeatedly. Each rollover introduces costs. And since futures prices often differ from spot prices—frequently trading at a premium—this process can create a persistent drag on returns. On top of this, leverage does not disappear over time. It simply compounds volatility. Daily price movements are amplified, which means gains and losses fluctuate in a way that does not behave like traditional long-term assets.

For short-term exposure, investors sometimes turn to other instruments such as **CFDs (contracts for difference)**. These do not involve ownership of the underlying asset. They **simply replicate its price movement over a short horizon**, with profit or loss determined by the difference between entry and exit. Options offer another alternative. If the trade fails, the loss is limited to the premium paid.

Unlike bonds, equities, or real estate, none of these instruments generate income. Their value depends entirely on price movement. For a more concrete breakdown of short-term commodity exposure, the appendices provide additional examples across major commodity categories. These sections are optional and not required for understanding the main framework.

## What this means for you in the long term

A much less risky alternative for individual investors is to use commodity funds designed to track commodity prices. However, this tracking is not perfect. Because many commodities are perishable or time-sensitive, fund providers—like individual investors—cannot hold physical inventories indefinitely[63]. They are therefore forced to roll futures contracts over time. This creates a structural limitation: over the long term, **these instruments, whether ETFs[64] or certificates, do not always replicate spot prices accurately. There is, however, one**

**notable exception: metals.**

**Another way to gain exposure to commodities is indirectly, through equities. Investors can buy shares in companies operating in the energy and materials sectors. These firms often benefit when commodity prices rise, while also distributing dividends, which adds an income component that direct commodity exposure does not provide.** This relationship is not uniform across all sectors. Coal, for example, is a notable exception. It faces significant structural headwinds, including regulatory pressure, the global energy transition, and increasing taxation. These factors reduce long-term visibility and make the sector more volatile and less attractive as a long-term investment, despite its sensitivity to commodity prices. **In the agricultural sector, investing in agri-food companies such as Nestlé, Unilever, or Danone will not necessarily lead to the expected price appreciation. In fact, these multinational groups are often negatively affected when raw material prices rise sharply.** Unlike oil majors such as ExxonMobil, BP, or TotalEnergies, which produce, process, and sell the underlying commodity, food companies are primarily buyers of raw materials. If the price of cocoa doubles, for example, the cost of producing chocolate increases significantly. Their only real response is their ability to pass on higher input costs to consumers through higher prices, a mechanism known as pricing power. However, this pricing power is generally much weaker than in the energy sector, largely due to differences in demand elasticity. For instance, a 20-cent increase in the price per liter of gasoline has little effect on consumption, as demand is relatively inelastic—individuals still need to drive to work and often have no immediate substitute. In contrast, a 20-cent increase in the price of bananas[65] is more difficult for consumers to accept, as they can more easily switch to alternative products. **The correlation is therefore stronger for trading companies[66], although their performance tends to reflect changes in margins more closely than direct movements in share prices.** The four largest agricultural trading companies in the world are Archer Daniels Midland, Bunge, Cargill, and the Louis Dreyfus Group, collectively known as the "ABCD" group. Of these, only the first two are publicly listed and therefore accessible to individual investors. **Another option is to invest in funds that own farmland and lease it to farmers. Although farmland generally generates lower returns than trading or processing activities, rising grain prices tend to increase land values over time, as well as rental income levels.**

# CHAPTER 17 :

## Gold, silver and other metals

*I*nvesting in metals has long been an important component of wealth management strategies. Historically associated with wealth and stability, certain metals are particularly attractive in periods marked by economic uncertainty, inflation, and geopolitical tensions. This includes gold and silver, as well as other industrial metals such as platinum, copper, iron, nickel, aluminum, lead, tin, and zinc. Gold [67]and silver[68] are the metals most sought after by investors. Because these two metals have been used as money for thousands of years, their long-term trends can be studied through historical price data.

For gold, the price per troy ounce was USD 18.93 in 1833; USD 18.99 in 1914; USD 20.63 in 1929; USD 33.85 in 1940; USD 40.62 in 1971; USD 615 in 1980; USD 279 in 2000; USD 871 in 2008; USD 1'668 in 2012; USD 1'268 in 2018; and approximately USD 4'300 today. This represents an annualized growth rate of approximately 2.85%. Starting the calculation from 1970, this increase is more than twice the observed inflation rate. **As a result, gold has historically demonstrated a strong ability to preserve purchasing power over time.** Its role in a wealth management strategy is primarily based on this characteristic. To illustrate, one can roughly assume a working life of around 40 years followed by approximately 20 years of retirement—a ratio of two to one. A strategy aimed at preserving purchasing power over the long term would imply that investing USD 300 per month during working life should, in principle, translate into approximately USD 600 per month in retirement purchasing power. Gold can play a role in this objective.

Its primary function is to provide protection against inflation. As such, **it tends to perform poorly during periods of positive real interest rates, but often rises during monetary shocks**, as observed in 1933 (the devaluation of the US dollar during the Great Depression) and in 1971 (the end of the Bretton Woods system amid the Vietnam War and expansionary fiscal policies). Its appeal lies in this behavior: as a **perceived safe-haven asset, gold tends to appreciate when confidence in fiat currency declines, particularly during periods of negative real interest rates. Conversely, when real interest rates rise, gold tends to underperform, even in environments of elevated inflation**[69]. As previously discussed, money functions as a store of value, but when this function is weakened, investors often turn to gold. In other words, when confidence in traditional currencies declines, the price of gold tends to rise—and this mechanism is not new. Even in the Roman Empire, gold acted as a safe haven when the Roman currency, the denarius, lost credibility. To finance military campaigns and public spending—such as under Nero—and later during periods of war and plague under Marcus Aurelius, authorities progressively reduced the metal content of coins in order to increase money supply. This gradual debasement was barely noticeable at first, until the denarius ultimately lost its credibility in the 3rd century BC[70]. At that point, only gold coins retained their value.

Silver has historically been less valuable than gold. In the Roman Empire[71], the gold-to-silver ratio was approximately 1:12. In Chinese empires[72], it typically ranged between 1:6 and 1:8, rarely exceeding 1:10. In the Americas, following large-scale silver production[73] by the Spanish in the 16th century, the ratio widened to between 1:15 and 1:18. Over the past century, this ratio has fluctuated significantly, ranging from approximately 1:20 (notably in 1920, 1970, and 1981) to as high as 1:100 (in 1941, 1991, 2020, and 2025). It has not sustainably fallen below

1:50 since the second half of the 1980s.

In terms of price history, the troy ounce of silver was valued at approximately USD 1.29 in 1792, according to the Coinage Act. This peg remained in place, with occasional exceptions, until 1873[74]. The price then declined to USD 0.50 per ounce in 1914, USD 0.35 in 1940, USD 1.64 in 1970, USD 32.75 in 1980, USD 5.04 in 2000, USD 17.38 in 2008, USD 31 in 2012, USD 23 in 2020, and approximately USD 72 today. This corresponds to an annualized growth rate of about 1.74% per year. Starting the calculation from 1970 yields a higher growth rate, but still around two percentage points lower than that of gold. **Silver has also experienced price surges during specific periods, but its behavior is generally more volatile and erratic.** The "Silver Thursday" episode of 1980 (see Appendix), triggered by the Hunt brothers' massive speculative positions, is a notable example. These dynamics can be explained by a smaller market size, lower liquidity, and a more limited number of participants, which makes silver prices more sensitive to large speculative flows.

To go further:

Both silver and gold have significant perceived value. They are associated with valuable materials, and the color of euro coins plays on this. The 1-euro and 2-euro coins, for example, although made primarily of a copper-based alloy, are silver and gold in color, so that people intuitively associate these colors with those metals. Here we see the symbolic power of gold and silver, which gives these coins an impression of value and prestige, even though they are not made of these precious metals. Conversely, the smaller coins (1, 2, and 5 centimes) made of copper-plated steel are red (the color of copper), visually reflecting their lower value. The same is true for many currencies around the world.

For U.S. dollars, the reasoning is the same: although all are made of a copper-based alloy, the gold-colored coins (1 USD) are perceived as more "solid" and valuable than the silver-colored coins (0.05; 0.10; 0.25, and 0.50 USD), which are themselves perceived as more "solid" and valuable than the copper-colored ones (0.01 USD). For cost reasons, coins are no longer made of silver as they were in the past, but the color has been retained so that people can immediately recognize the coin's value (associated with a small, medium, or large denomination).

**As for the other metals and minerals mentioned, they have never historically been considered safe-haven assets. Nevertheless, some have experienced significant price increases over the past thirty years. Among them, copper and iron are often regarded as the most attractive.** Copper is closely linked to electrification[75], telecommunications infrastructure, and the energy transition, while iron remains central to steel production, and therefore to construction and industrial activity. Each metal has specific industrial uses and applications. Nickel has gained importance in batteries and stainless steel production. Aluminum[76] benefits from its lightness and versatility, while tin[77], lead[78], and zinc[79] have more specialized industrial uses. **These metals are primarily driven by global demand—and therefore by economic growth**—in sectors such as infrastructure, construction, transportation, and manufacturing. As a result, their historical performance is closely tied to the economic cycle, mining supply, and major structural shifts, particularly the energy transition and the development of green technologies. For example, copper is essential for electrical infrastructure and renewable energy systems, making it a strategic metal in the context of climate transition.Investing in metals can be done in several ways. Physical ownership provides[80] direct exposure to the asset but comes with storage and security constraints. Exchange-traded funds (ETFs) offer a simpler and more liquid form of exposure. Futures contracts, on the other hand, are generally reserved for professional investors due to their complexity and embedded leverage.

It is also important to note that, unlike bonds or equities, these metals do not generate income and do not provide any form of passive return. **Their main value lies in capital protection and portfolio diversification rather than income generation.**

**This diversification role extends to the broader commodities asset class,** which has historically performed well during periods of unexpected inflation—often when traditional asset classes such as stocks and bonds tend to underperform, as shown in the study by Gorton and Rouwenhorst[81]. Commodities tend to behave differently from financial assets because their value is tied directly to the physical economy rather than to cash flows or discount rates. As a result, they can act as a counterbalance when inflation shocks disrupt the usual relationships between stocks, bonds, and interest rates. In that sense, **commodities exist in a portfolio for a simple reason: they tend to perform when other assets do not. Knowing when that moment arrives is the whole question.**

# PART VI

## Stocks: The Long Game

# CHAPTER 18 :

## What a stock actually represents

With emergency savings and a primary residence, you've already secured a significant portion of your financial future. The same is broadly true for a combination of savings and bonds, although the question of housing after retirement may still remain. In either case, the essentials are covered. What comes next is no longer about protection. It is about growth. When you invest in rental real estate, that is precisely what you are doing. Equities are another. Why do investors turn to stocks? Because few asset classes have created as much wealth over long periods of time.

But what exactly is a stock? At its core, a stock represents ownership in a company. A company is an organization founded by a group of individuals (or a single individual) who pool resources[82] in order to conduct business and generate profits[83]. Every company has owners. When ownership is divided into shares, each share represents a legal claim on a portion of the company's equity. Owning a share therefore means owning a small part of the business itself. In this sense, a stock is nothing more than a fractional ownership interest in a company. The distinction between a *share* and *stock* is the following:

- that a stock is easily transferable. Selling it is very flexible, often unrestricted except under specific clauses, whereas;
- the sale of a share is more regulated and often limited by internal agreements. In practice, this means that the agreement of all shareholders is mandatory to sell to a

third party, with a possible right of first refusal.

In the United States, the terms *stocks* and *shares* are generally used interchangeably. The distinction is mostly relevant in legal or corporate contexts, particularly when referring to ownership interests in certain types of companies. For practical purposes, we will focus on stocks.

Stocks are arguably the investment vehicle par excellence for most investors, largely because they are easy to buy and sell. This liquidity is valuable. All else being equal, economists generally observe that assets that can be traded quickly and easily tend to command higher valuations than comparable illiquid assets.

In simple terms[84], owning a stock grants three main rights: the right to vote on certain corporate matters, the right to receive dividends while the company operates, and a claim on any remaining assets if the company is liquidated after all debts have been repaid.

There are two ways to become an owner of a company. You can create the company yourself, or you can purchase shares from an existing owner. In the latter case, the money you invest does not go to the company itself but to the shareholder selling the shares.

Because a company exists to generate profits for its owners, it typically holds a wide variety of assets. These may include financial assets such as cash, bonds, stocks, or cryptocurrencies; tangible assets such as inventory, raw materials, land, or real estate; and intangible assets such as patents, intellectual property, or goodwill. It may also own machinery, equipment, artwork, or other assets with economic value. A stock represents a fractional ownership interest in those assets and in the future profits they may generate. The size of that ownership depends on how many shares you hold. If a company has 100 shares outstanding and you own one share, you own 1% of the company. But owning 1% of a small local restaurant is very different from owning 1% of a global restaurant chain. The value of your ownership, the dividends you may receive, and your share of any liquidation proceeds will differ accordingly. It is therefore perfectly logical that the price investors are willing to pay also differs.

**When a stock is publicly traded, determining its value appears straightforward. Its market price can be checked instantly on a phone or computer.** As long as the market is open, a quoted price is always available. That price is determined by supply and demand and reflects the most recent transaction between a willing buyer and a willing seller. Under normal market conditions, investors can generally expect to buy or sell near that price.

**When a company is not publicly traded**, valuation becomes less obvious. Without a continuous market, how can a price be determined? **The closest reference is often the price of recent transactions involving the company's shares.** The logic remains the same: value is inferred from what someone was willing to pay. The more recent the transaction, the more reliable that reference tends to be. As time passes, however, the last transaction price becomes less of a benchmark and more of a starting point for negotiation.

Public stock exchanges process thousands of transactions every day involving large numbers of participants. As a result, prices are constantly updated and generally provide a reliable estimate of market value. Private markets, by contrast, operate differently. Transactions are less frequent, the pool of potential buyers is smaller, transparency is lower[85], and prices depend more heavily on negotiation.

For this reason, investors often rely on valuation methods designed to estimate a reasonable range of value rather than a single precise figure. These approaches—discussed in greater detail in the appendix—may incorporate intrinsic value estimates, expected returns, comparable companies, liquidity conditions, timing, and investor sentiment. Ultimately, however, value and price are not the same thing. A valuation can be estimated, but only an actual transaction reveals the price with certainty.

In practical terms, when investing in publicly traded stocks, only a few variables truly matter: **the price you pay when you buy, the price you receive when you sell, and any dividends[86] collected along the way.** Everything else ultimately feeds into those three elements.

| Year 0 | Year 1 | Year 2 | .... | Final year |
|---|---|---|---|---|
| Purchase price | Dividend 1 | Dividend 2 | .... | Exit price |

Some elements of an investment are within your control, while others are not. The variables you can control include the price you pay and the most recent dividend received. What lies beyond your control—and can only be estimated—are future dividends and the price at which you will eventually sell. As a result, the shorter your investment horizon, the more your outcome depends on the exit price. There simply is not enough time for dividends to accumulate and compound meaningfully. Over longer periods, however, dividends become increasingly important. Given enough time, they can represent a substantial portion of total return.

Ultimately, when you buy a stock, you are investing in what the company will become over time. This is simply the nature of equity ownership. A share is not just a ticker symbol or a fluctuating market price—it is a proportional ownership stake in a real business. Over the long run, the value of your investment will therefore tend to reflect the company's underlying performance.

To go further

A stock's price is often expressed as a multiple of its earnings. In this context, the company's market capitalization is said to be equal to X times its earnings. This is the principle behind the Price-to-Earnings Ratio (or P/E). This ratio is widely used in the stock market because it allows for easy comparison of companies.

For example, if a share is worth 100 euros and earnings per share are 5 euros, then the P/E ratio is 20 (100 ÷ 5). The market is thus paying 20 times the company's annual earnings. This means that if earnings remain the same, it would theoretically take 20 years to "recoup" the price paid. When calculating the Price-Earnings Ratio, we realize that two companies in the same sector with similar earnings can have very different P/E ratios. This is because the price an investor pays does not actually take into account only current earnings, but also incorporates future prospects (profit growth, predictability of expectations, and the ability to become a dominant player in the sector). Thus, for a company with a P/E ratio of 40 times annual earnings, the market is no longer paying just for the present, but also—and above all—for the expected future. This can signify extraordinary potential, or conversely, a massive speculative bubble. An investor should therefore not ask whether the P/E ratio is high, but whether future prospects justify it.

# CHAPTER 19 :

## Index funds vs. active management: what the studies say

*W*hen it comes to **day trading by retail investors, the research is clear. The vast majority of retail investors lose money.** Fewer than a quarter break even, and only around 1% to 5% are consistently profitable after costs. Professionals (such as traders at banks or hedge funds) may achieve better results, but their approach and operating conditions are fundamentally different. By virtue of their position, they have access to substantial liquidity, which, combined with advanced infrastructure (high-performance servers[87], low-latency systems, and algorithmic trading), allows them to exploit very small price discrepancies—sometimes thousands of times per day. They do not typically claim to "predict" the future. Instead, they often seek technical or structural gains by identifying inefficiencies, executing short-term arbitrage, and relying on quantitative models. The scale of resources involved is entirely different. So are the costs[88], constraints, and execution capabilities. **For a retail investor, buying and selling every day based on news is the surest way to lose money. By contrast, the most effective long-term strategy is simply to invest by passively tracking market trends.** Studies[89] have reached this conclusion for many years. Once management fees are taken into account, passively tracking the S&P 500 U.S. stock index outperforms the vast majority of U.S. asset managers, regardless of the reference period or time horizon considered. The S&P 500 index therefore outperforms

78% of asset managers over a 1-year time horizon; 67% over 3 years; 88% over 5 years; 85% over 10 years; and 89% over 15 years. Paying high "performance fees" does not change this result. It does not necessarily translate into improved net returns for investors[90]. **In other words, if you are looking for performance, "do not look for the needle in the haystack. Buy the whole haystack," as per John Bogle**, founder of Vanguard and creator of the first retail index fund in 1976. Don't focus on a few specific stocks; buy them all at once. This is what an index fund (ETF, or Exchange-Traded Fund) allows you to do. Its purpose is to replicate the performance of its benchmark index[91] by holding all the stocks that make up that index. This is also what Warren Buffett himself recommends. Considered the greatest investor in history, he advises 99% of investors to hold a low-cost S&P 500 ETF[92] for 30 years. Do not watch the price. Do not sell during a crisis. Just total diversification and time. That is the recipe for success.

In times of crisis, you can even add to your portfolio. Peter Lynch, who managed the Fidelity Magellan Fund for over 20 years, puts it this way: "I've found that when the market is down and you invest wisely in funds, you'll end up satisfied. You won't achieve that just by reading 'It's time to buy.'" This observation regarding the underperformance of active management also holds true for all other studied countries, namely Canada, Mexico, Brazil[93], Chile, Europe, the Middle East, South Africa, Japan, and Australia. If you want to focus on a particular country or geographic region, you should also opt for a passive index fund, since markets offer few structural opportunities[94] for active management (individual stock selection, or "stock picking"), and virtually none in the long term.

Data shows that funds in the top quartile (among the top 25% performers) over a given period are only slightly more likely than chance to remain in the top quartile over the next period (*S&P SPIVA Persistence Scorecard*, 2023). This can be explained by a phenomenon known as "reversion to the mean."

What outperforms at a given time (management style, sector trends, thematic focus) may underperform later. In other words, the outcome is broadly the same across the board. Since things are well made, **the most effective approach is also the simplest: buy a broad index ETF and hold it for the long term.**

# CHAPTER 20:

## What we can reasonably expect from it

*T*o appreciate what stocks can deliver over time, consider a few recent examples. Over the last decade, the S&P 500 —the benchmark index of the 500 largest publicly traded companies in the United States—has generated an annualized return of approximately 13.7%. Over the same period, the MSCI World, which includes more than 1,300 companies across 23 developed countries, returned slightly above 13% per year, while the MSCI ACWI, which also includes emerging markets[95], produced a return only slightly below that figure. These are remarkable results.

give you an idea of the performance one can expect from investing in the stock market, the S&P 500, the benchmark index of the American market (the 500 largest publicly traded companies in the country), has posted an annualized return of 13.68% over the last 10 years. Meanwhile, the MSCI World (1'310 companies from 23 developed countries worldwide) has posted an annualized return slightly above 13% over the last 10 years; while the MSCI ACWI (2'514 companies from 23 developed and 24 emerging countries) has posted a return slightly below this 13% figure over the last decade. These figures are impressive.

Looking further back, the picture remains equally compelling. **Over the past century, the US stock market has delivered annualized returns of roughly 10% per year (Dimson, Marsh & Staunton, 2002; Credit Suisse *Global Investment Returns Yearbook*, 2021).** Few asset classes have matched this long-term performance. The United States has been one of the most successful developed markets in history, and that trend has continued into the 21st century. However, the outcome becomes clearer as the time horizon expands. In the short-term, they are highly unpredictable. As Benjamin Graham reminds readers in *The Intelligent Investor*, investors should be prepared for periods in which their stocks decline "by the equivalent of one-third or more of their peak at various times over the next five years." Such declines are not anomalies. They are part of the experience. This is why the investment horizon matters so much. The edge of equities comes from time. **Investing in the stock market is a long-term commitment, but you don't know exactly how long you will have to wait to benefit from this historically observed performance.** To give you an idea, the S&P 500 was essentially flat from 1901 to 1921, and it took more than two decades to regain its previous peak following the crash of 1929. After the dot-com bubble burst in the early 2000s, recovery took roughly seven years; about five years following the Global Financial Crisis of 2008; only a few months for the Covid-19 crash of 2020. By contrast, investors in Japan waited approximately thirty-five years for the market to reclaim its 1989 peak. Thus, the long term can be very long.

The lesson is straightforward. Stocks have historically rewarded patience, but they have rarely rewarded impatience. **When you invest in equities, you should only commit capital that you will not need for many years, and be prepared to bear the consequences over time.** The challenge is therefore not simply choosing good investments. It is remaining invested long enough to benefit from them. Avoid panic selling during downturns. Avoid excessive trading that gradually erodes returns. Give compounding time to work. Time, in the stocks exchange, is often what turns average results into exceptional ones.

To go further:

Stocks generally underperform during periods of high inflation. An inflation rate approaching double digits has a negative impact on stock performance. Real returns (after adjusting for inflation) often even turn negative once this threshold is crossed. If inflation is specific to your country and your currency is the problem, you can always turn to a stronger foreign currency. Otherwise, other solutions must be considered. Metal commodities like gold can help you in certain circumstances (see the dedicated chapter).

Another useful way to measure stock market performance is to compare it with government bonds. The equity risk premium measures the difference in return between these two asset classes: equities on one side, and risk-free assets such as government bonds on the other. When making long-term comparisons, long-term government bonds (10 years or more) are typically used as the benchmark.

The logic is similar to that of credit spreads between bonds with different ratings. Just as a BBB-rated bond offers a higher yield than an AAA-rated bond to compensate for higher default risk, equities are expected to deliver higher returns than government bonds because they are riskier and more uncertain. A key difference, however, is that credit spreads are known in advance, while the equity risk premium is uncertain and only observable ex post. It can be estimated for the future, but never guaranteed. Aswath Damodaran of New York University Stern, for example, regularly publishes country-specific estimates of implied equity risk premiums. It can also be observed in hindsight.

This spread naturally varies across countries and time periods. In the United States, it has averaged around 4.4 percentage points between 1900 and 2020. In practical terms, this means that U.S. equities outperformed U.S. government bonds by 4.4% per year on average over this period. Here again, the United States stands out for its high equity risk premium (like Japan or Germany), which has historically been higher[96] than that of other "developed" countries. That said, past averages should not be interpreted as forecasts. For instance, while the long-term premium was high in Japan and Germany over the last century, it was only around 1 percentage point[97] between 1973 and 2011. Japan in particular experienced a prolonged period of underperformance from the 1990s through the mid-2000s. The equity risk premium, while positive in theory, can therefore compress significantly, and in some cases become zero or even negative under specific conditions.

Academic research shows[98] that, in reality, everything depends on the economic environment. **Equity tends to outperform government bonds in most environments, with one major exception: periods of severe deflation.** In such regimes, real returns on bonds can exceed those of equities. Typical examples include the Great Depression of the 1930s in the United States and Japan's "lost decades" beginning in the 1990s. This does not refer to short-lived price declines following financial crises, but to persistent deflationary spirals in which falling prices and weak demand reinforce each other over time. This is one reason why global diversification remains important, as it helps reduce exposure to country-specific deflationary shocks. Warren Buffett, for example, has often advocated for S&P 500 index exposure, reflecting a view that sustained deflation in the United States is highly unlikely given the institutional response since the Great Depression. The Federal Reserve has consistently acted aggressively to prevent such outcomes, even at the risk of higher inflation[99] later on.

It is also worth noting that the entry point plays a major role in long-term equity returns. The higher the price paid at entry, the lower the expected return over the following decade. This relationship has been widely documented. One way to frame it is through valuation multiples: when you buy a company at 20 times earnings and later sell it at the same multiple, your return will largely depend on earnings growth and dividends received during the holding period. Assuming a 50% payout ratio[100], this could translate into an annualized pre-tax return of around 6.5% with 4% earnings growth, and approximately 8.5% with 6% growth. By contrast, if you buy at 30 times earnings and sell ten years later at 20 times, the effect of multiple compression significantly reduces returns: a 4% earnings growth rate may result in less than 2% annualized return, and a 6% growth rate in just under 4%. Conversely, buying at low multiples and exiting at higher ones compounds both earnings growth and valuation expansion. The table below summarizes how annualized equity returns vary as a function of these two drivers:

| P/E Evolution | Profit growth rate | | | | | | |
|---|---|---|---|---|---|---|---|
| | -2% | 0% | 2% | 4% | 6% | 8% | 10% |
| 10 to 10 | 3.00 | 5.00 | 7.00 | 9.00 | 11.00 | 13.00 | 15.00 |
| 10 to 15 | 6.31 | 8.39 | 10.47 | 12.56 | 14.63 | 16.72 | 18.80 |
| 10 to 20 | 8.84 | 10.98 | 13.13 | 15.27 | 17.41 | 19.55 | 21.70 |
| 15 to 15 | 1.33 | 3.33 | 5.33 | 7.33 | 9.33 | 11.33 | 13.33 |
| 15 to 20 | 3.82 | 5.88 | 7.93 | 9.99 | 12.05 | 14.41 | 16.17 |
| 15 to 25 | 5.84 | 7.95 | 10.05 | 12.16 | 14.26 | 16.36 | 18.47 |
| 20 to 20 | 0.50 | 2.5 | 4.50 | 6.50 | 8.50 | 10.50 | 12.50 |

| 20 to 25 | 2.49 | 4.53 | 6.57 | 8.62 | 10.67 | 12.71 | 14.76 |
|---|---|---|---|---|---|---|---|
| 25 to 25 | 0.00 | 2.00 | 4.00 | 6.00 | 8.00 | 10.00 | 12.00 |
| 25 to 30 | 1.65 | 3.69 | 5.73 | 7.76 | 9.8 | 11.84 | 13.87 |
| 30 to 30 | -0.33 | 1.67 | 3.67 | 5.67 | 7.67 | 9.67 | 11.67 |
| 30 to 25 | -1.96 | 0.00 | 1.96 | 3.93 | 5.89 | 7.86 | 9.82 |
| 30 to 20 | -3.89 | -1.97 | -0.05 | 1.87 | 3.79 | 5.71 | 7.63 |
| 25 to 20 | -1.96 | 0.00 | 1.96 | 3.91 | 5.87 | 7.82 | 9.78 |
| 25 to 15 | -4.36 | -2.46 | -0.56 | 1.34 | 3.24 | 5.14 | 7.04 |
| 20 to 15 | -1.94 | 0.00 | 1.94 | 3.89 | 5.83 | 7.77 | 9.72 |
| 20 to 10 | -5.15 | -3.28 | -1.42 | 0.45 | 2.32 | 4.19 | 6.05 |
| 15 to 10 | -1.92 | 0.00 | 1.92 | 3.84 | 5.76 | 7.96 | 9.61 |

*A similar table, this time covering a 30-year time horizon, is included in the Appendix. The case including taxation is also addressed there, assuming a tax rate of 30% on both dividends and capital gains.*

In this context, tracking long-term bond yields, whether on government or corporate bonds, helps you to understand your position within the broader investment landscape. Comparing bond yields with stock market valuations also provides useful insights into which asset class appears more attractive. One of the main advantages of bonds is that their expected return is largely known in advance. This allows investors to directly compare the return offered by bonds with the return expected from equities and to assess which investment opportunity is more attractive at any given time. The fact that bond yields are relatively certain and observable from the outset is the greatest strength of this asset class.

Regarding stocks investments made at high valuations, it is generally observed that they tend to reduce future returns, unless this effect is offset by strong earnings growth.

# CHAPTER 21 :

## Stock picking: the factors value, quality, growth and momentum

*H*ere are the things you need to know if you still want to do stock picking. In the short term, stock price movements are driven by company-specific events and broader macroeconomic conditions (such as monetary policy or the regulatory environment). Below is a list of events that generally have a positive impact on stock prices: acceleration of organic growth; a cut in key interest rates by the central bank; a successful acquisition; entry into a new high-growth market; improved margins; management change suggesting better capital allocation; significant share buyback; credit rating upgrade by a rating agency; inclusion in a major index. Conversely, the following events tend to negatively impact stock prices: disappointment regarding growth; loss of a major contract; increase in key interest rates by the central bank; visible technological disruption; governance scandal; profit warning.

You are therefore highly exposed to news about the company itself, as well as to relatively detailed financial performance indicators. **This makes it essential—unless you are willing to take a gamble—to have a solid understanding of the company you are investing in.** This means knowing what it does, how it generates revenue, and how its business model works, as well as understanding its financial health and key performance metrics. For the market caps tracked by analysts[101], it can also be useful to look at the positioning of major funds operating in the sector you are interested in.

Over time horizons ranging from a few months to a year, analysts' consensus tends to be relatively accurate in forecasting these indicators, often even before companies publish their earnings. This consensus is built by teams of analysts who study published reports[102], build detailed financial models to project future results, and maintain close contact with industry participants to detect early signals of business activity—including management and suppliers. In this environment, your informational advantage is relatively limited. As for pure price speculation, you are also operating at a disadvantage, since professional investors (banks, hedge funds, pension funds) typically rely on Reuters or Bloomberg terminals—costing tens of thousands of dollars per user per year—to access real-time data and highly granular market information, as well as industry chat platforms[103] that facilitate the rapid exchange of information and sentiment across the market.

**For this reason, it is generally better to focus on a time horizon of at least one year or more.** The reason is simple: the longer the horizon, the less precise short-term analyst forecasts become. At the same time, this allows more time for a sound investment thesis to play out. Provided, of course, that the thesis is correct—because a flawed analysis does not disappear over time; it compounds into a slow loss. The key is therefore to combine analytical rigor with patience and discipline. Avoiding making a choice by default helps enormously.

To integrate stock picking into a structured and predictable long-term strategy, it is useful to understand that each stock can be classified into a specific category (often referred to as a factor). Here are the five main ones:

- Value. These are stocks that are undervalued by the market. They are cheap relative to their fundamentals. The idea is that the market is temporarily undervaluing them and that the gap will close;
- Quality is for profitable, stable, and low-debt compan-

ies. You know they are here to stay and that their market share in the sector is not going to collapse overnight; you are even betting on the strengthening of this dominant position.

- *Growth* represents stocks with strong revenue or profit growth. You are therefore paying for a company in full development. The idea is that the valuation will increase, and that the price paid today will be minimal compared to what it will be tomorrow;
- High dividends are mature companies that generate a lot of cash and distribute it regularly to shareholders. The idea is to generate stable income, like with bonds, while benefiting from the share price increase and the expected excess performance associated with stocks (risk premium). Especially in retirement;

A dynamic element may also have been added,

- Momentum. Studies by Narasimhan Jegadeesh and Sheridan Titman in 1993 showed that buying stocks that have risen sharply and selling those that have fallen the most generates excess performance over the following 3 to 12 months. The idea is that there is a tendency due to inertia in the processing of information.

These factors have already been extensively studied in the past, which means it is possible to understand the conditions under which they tend to perform well, and those in which they are less effective. Because they are based on long-term empirical observations, they also provide a reasonable sense of what to expect in terms of returns. That said, they are not a "magic formula." Instead, their main value is that they help reduce reliance on intuition, storytelling, or "gut feeling" when selecting individual stocks, adding a more structured layer to the decision-making process.

It is also worth noting that ETFs exist which replicate these factors within major indices such as the S&P 500 or NASDAQ in the United States, or the Euro Stoxx 50 in Europe, depending on the market exposure you choose. The next six sections are dedicated to analyzing them in detail.

## Finding an undervalued company

In this scenario, the reasoning is clear, and a relatively simple parallel can be drawn with real estate: it would be like buying an apartment at an attractive price. An asset, even an imperfect one, purchased at a low price can indeed become an excellent investment. How can this be achieved in the financial markets?

We then seek to determine its book value (the figure that indicates what the company would be worth if all its assets were sold and all its debts repaid). For example, if a company is valued at 100 million dollars on the stock market and you find a book value of 80 million dollars means you're buying it below its actual value. The greater the discount, the theoretically greater your profit potential. Buying shares on this basis is therefore a gamble: hoping the market will recognize this difference and close the gap before selling; or risking being trapped by a company that will only weaken over time. Because a company withdiscountIt can be a trap if profits collapse .**This method was popularized by Benjamin Graham,** which applied it to its extreme (seeking massive discounts of sometimes 50% and more), **made his fortune in the 1930s-1960s**, before inspiring many imitators (including Warren Buffett at the beginning of his Berkshire Hathaway fund).

However, today, a company's value relies less than in the past on tangible, heavy assets (heavy industry, factories, buildings, warehouses). The value of companies is increasingly relying on its intangible assets (reputation, software, data, know-how). In a context where market value is almost always higher than book value, determining whether a company is undervalued relative to its fundamentals is implemented in ways that vary considerably among professionals. The metrics currently used by MCSI (formerly Morgan Stanley Capital International) to determine this are:

- the ratio between the company's market capitalization and its book value, called Price to Book value (P/B) ;
- the Price Earnings Ratio (P/E), or rather, for MCSI, the Forward Price to Earnings Ratio (Fwd P/E). It differs in that it is based on future earnings;
- The Enterprise Value / Operating Cash Flows (EV/CFO) ratio, which focuses on the company's cash flows[104].

These three metrics are weighted to produce an overall score for the company, which can then be compared to others. This can even extend to investing in companies emerging from Chapter 11 bankruptcy in the United States. In such cases, the problem must stem from debt rather than the business model. This is because debt can be restructured, whereas a business model cannot.

This value-investing approach is highly valued by activist funds that take (at least partial) control of the company. If the stock market fails to recognize this value differential, you always have the option to sell the assets you've previously identified, or to pressure management to do so. In a way, this provides a safety net known in advance (real estate for Blackstone during the Hilton acquisition). The goal of the transaction may be directly to resell the assets and realize a capital gain. But it can just as easily fit into a broader strategy, such as seeking to improve the company's margins—which are lower than those of its competitors[105]—refocusing it on its profitable activities (Daniel Seth Loeb via the Third Point fund), redistributing excess cash (Carl Icahn), reducing unnecessary expenses, and so on. One strategy does not preclude another.

To go further :

You may also be interested in assets that the market has overlooked—such as real estate that has not been revalued for a long time, dormant patents that have fallen off the radar, or mispriced legal risks where potential liabilities or fines are misunderstood[106]. In these cases, the key question is whether the true value is higher than what is currently reflected in the price or the book value.

However, markets can let it unseen for extended periods. A mispricing alone is often not enough to close the gap. For value to be realized, a catalyst is usually required. As an independent investor, simply identifying and publicizing the opportunity is rarely sufficient[107]. In most cases, it remains only a signal. Nor does an individual investor typically have the financial capacity to force convergence between price and value. Doing so can require substantial resources and resilience. For example, Bill Ackman's position against Herbalife through Pershing Square Capital Management involved approximately $1 billion in capital and required the ability to withstand significant drawdowns before the thesis played out —or failed. For this reason, the catalyst must generally be external, credible, and independent of the investor's own actions. Without it, even a correct analysis may take a very long time to be reflected in market prices.

## Focus on quality

Quality is for companies that are evaluated solely based on qualitative factors. In short, you're looking for a profitable company with very little debt and consistently improving results over time. Here are the metrics used by MCSI to achieve this:

- le ratio Return on Equity[108](ROE) which shows the efficiency of the company's investments in generating results;
- le ratio Debt to Equity[109] (D/E) which shows its financial indebtedness;
- and the variability of annual results over the last five

years to account for whether revenue growth has been very consistent.

can also be added (in a logic similar to that of Warren Buffett, although not present in the MSCI criteria),

- stable or expanding operating margins;
- cash flow metrics that reveal the truly distributable profit.

When the focus is on quality, the entry price becomes less central. This has an important implication: the investment horizon tends to lengthen. Over longer periods, the price paid at entry matters less, because time allows fundamentals to drive returns. Consider a stock priced at $100, increasing by 6% per year and paying $2 in annual dividends. This results in an annualized return of approximately 7.9% over a 3-year horizon. However, if the entry price rises to $120, the return drops sharply to around 1.4%. Over a longer horizon, the picture changes. Over 20 years, the same assumptions produce a return of about 7.2% when purchased at $100, and still around 6.1% when purchased at $120. The difference is clear: over short periods, paying too much has a major impact on performance. Over long periods, that effect is gradually absorbed by time and compounding. This is because high-quality companies have time to create value. And over longer horizons, investors participate in that value creation, even if their entry point was not optimal.

This is why, in the case of quality stocks, price isn't even an official criterion. The key question becomes what allows this to be true in the first place. **The answer lies in identifying companies that are leaders in their field—and are likely to remain so over time. In other words, businesses with durable strength and resilience.** This is where Charlie Munger, vice chairman of Berkshire Hathaway, introduced the concept of economic "moats." His core idea is simple: there is no such thing as a static moat. A moat that does not widen gradually tends, over time, to narrow. From this perspective, paying a premium can be justified if the company possesses a durable competitive advantage —whether through distribution networks, network effects, or ecosystems that are difficult to replicate. Examples often cited include companies such as Coca-Cola, Meta (formerly Facebook), and Apple. For these types of businesses, the exact entry point becomes less critical, especially under a long-term, buy-and-hold assumption. An excessive focus on price alone can even lead investors to miss opportunities when the underlying moat is genuinely strong. In this framework, time works in favor of exceptional companies and against mediocre ones to use his expression. The key condition is that the competitive advantage must be durable and not easily eroded within a few years, since in effect the investor is betting on a generation of outcomes rather than a short cycle. Strong brand power, near-emotional customer loyalty, perceived reliability, and pricing power—the ability to raise prices without losing demand—are concrete manifestations of such a moat.

That said, few people could have predicted 20 years in advance the collapse of the CD market and its impact on media conglomerates (Vivendi, Sony), the rise of the internet and its consequences for directory services (Yellow Pages), e-commerce's impact on retail (Sears), streaming and its effect on the audiovisual sector (Warner Bros. Discovery), the shift to digital rendering disposable cameras obsolete (Kodak), smartphones replacing cell phones (Nokia, BlackBerry), and so on. **Hence the need to remain vigilant.** In most of these situations, the crucial factor is the degree to which these large groups adapt, rather than the disruptive factor itself. While some companies have managed to navigate these shifts more or less successfully to minimize the damage, others, on the other hand, have simply disappeared. It is better here not to put all your eggs in one basket and to diversify. If one fails, the others will cushion the blow. **When well-diversified, quality stocks tend to follow a long-term trajectory relatively similar to that of the indices, with greater resilience during crises and a slower recovery once the shock has passed.**

## Combining quality with an attractive entry price

A company can be excellent, but if that quality is already widely recognized, the stock is often expensive. This naturally raises questions about valuation. The idea is to combine two elements: investing in high-quality businesses, but not at any price. This often requires waiting for an entry point. That opportunity can be short-lived or more persistent. It may come from disappointing results at competitors, which unfairly drag the stock down by association despite unchanged fundamentals. Or it may result from a broader market shock—an unexpected event that triggers a sharp but temporary repricing.

This is what happened when Berkshire Hathaway built its position in American Express in the 1960s, after a scandal led to a significant drop in the share price. The key point was that the issue was temporary. Customers quickly moved on, the company's core business remained intact, and its reputation proved resilient over time. The problem was external to the business itself, not a reflection of its underlying quality.

One could also cite the example of Volkswagen AG, whose share price was cut in half within six months following the "Dieselgate" scandal. In this case, the issue originated within the company itself, rather than from an external shock. As a result, the impact went beyond short-term sentiment: the brand's image was significantly damaged, and trust was meaningfully weakened. While this represented a serious reputational and governance crisis, it did not threaten the company's existence.

The lesson for us is the following: what was done with American Express does not resemble what could have been done with Volkswagen. In the case of American Express, the opportunity came from a temporary external dislocation in sentiment, while the underlying business remained fundamentally unchanged. With Volkswagen, the situation is more complex, as the issue originated within the company itself and affected core elements such as governance and trust. The episode left lasting scars on its perception, even if Volkswagen still exists today and has since recovered part of its standing, gradually regaining strength over time. This distinction matters: one case reflects a mispricing driven by perception, the other a deeper reassessment of intrinsic quality.

We can see that over the course of half a century, Berkshire Hathaway's approach has evolved significantly. It has moved from a pure deep-value strategy over short horizons (such as Dempster Mill), to a virtually open-ended investment horizon focused on high-quality companies purchased at a discount (American Express[110]). It then shifted toward a balance between entry price and long-term potential (Coca-Cola[111]), before increasingly emphasizing business fundamentals and future earnings power (Apple[112]). **This evolution suggests that there is no single universal framework. Adaptation to context appears to be the consistent principle rather than adherence to a fixed formula.**

Because no single mathematical model is universally accepted, other approaches can also be used. Another useful example is Joel Greenblatt's framework, which combines two key ratios: earnings yield[113], to assess whether a company is attractively priced, and return on invested capital[114] (ROIC), to evaluate how efficiently it allocates resources. These two dimensions are closely related. Together, they link valuation and quality into a single, pragmatic investment lens, as outlined in *The Little Book That Beats the Market*.

## Aiming for growth

Here, you are targeting high-growth companies. The idea is to identify companies capable of growing faster than the market. The criteria used by MSCI to identify these companies are:

- the long-term trend in revenue per share growth;
- the current internal growth rate, which reflects the company's ability to expand using only its own resources;
- the long-term trend in earnings per share (EPS) growth;
- the projected short-term EPS growth rate;
- the projected long-term EPS growth rate.

Here again, the entry price isn't the primary focus, because if a company experiences significant growth over a long period, its future valuation will be multiplied, and the current purchase price becomes secondary. An expensive company becomes cheap if profits skyrocket. What you're buying here is a long-term growth trajectory.

**In recent stock market history, the big winners have often been in this category. Amazon, NVIDIA, and Tesla have long seemed "overpriced", with enormous P/E ratios, sometimes without any profit.** Yet growth ultimately exceeded expectations. The focus is primarily on a surge in future profits. A pure "growth" perspective therefore accepts extreme valuations if the growth potential appears exceptional.**You must also be prepared to accept more volatility given that you are highly dependent on future expectations.**The slightest interference (fall in results, rise in interest rates via its impact on the discount rate) strongly impacts these shares since a large part of their value comes from very distant profits.

## Combining growth and a reasonable price

To avoid this pitfall, a price component can be reintroduced. This reintroduces the concept of a margin of safety on the price paid. This is the concept of GARP (Growth At a Reasonable Price). You want a growth stock, but not at any price. The idea is to first select the companies with the highest growth scores, and then:

- A first filter is based on price relative to growth. This is closely aligned with Peter Lynch's approach and his PEG ratio[115] framework. The idea is not simply to avoid expensive companies, but to assess whether the price is justified by future growth. This requires an underlying assumption: that the company's growth is relatively stable and predictable. In turn, this implies understanding the business itself—whether growth is structural, cyclical, or temporary. The framework is not well suited to highly cyclical companies, where earnings fluctuate too sharply to be meaningfully projected. As an illustration, a company growing at 20% annually with a P/E ratio of 30 may still be considered attractive if that growth is sustainable over time. In this case, the investor's role is not to trade in and out, but to remain invested as long as the growth trajectory holds.

- A second step is to apply a "tilt" approach—adjusting exposure based on both price and quality factors. Price metrics include forward P/E, price-to-book, and other valuation indicators. Quality is assessed through profitability and balance sheet strength, such as return on equity, low leverage, and earnings stability. The key distinction is that a growth company is not simply one that grows quickly. It is one that can sustain growth in a profitable and financially sound way. In other words, growth must be durable. This tilting approach also helps avoid "growth traps"—companies whose revenues expand rapidly but are driven more by narrative than fundamentals. A seductive narrative (storytelling) and enthusiasm of the markets can mask weak underlying economics, such as poor cash generation, excessive leverage, or deteriorating unit economics. The result is growth that looks compelling on the surface but is not sustainable over time.

**The GARP approach tends to work best when investors move beyond the largest companies by market capitalization[116]. Its strengths become more visible in the small-cap segment.** Here, the potential for outperformance is higher, partly because information is less efficiently priced and opportunities are less widely analyzed. If you're willing to take the risk, these are the segments you should focus on. That said, **there is no guarantee of beating the S&P 500, which remains the benchmark for the U.S. equity market.**

To learn more:

In the small-cap market, the objective is often to identify something the market has not yet priced in. The opportunity exists because, by definition, fewer analysts and investors are paying attention to smaller companies. In that context, an investor's edge comes less from access to data than from interpretation. It is the ability to notice signals that may be overlooked by professionals sitting in front of terminals—or even by systems processing vast amounts of information. This often comes down to personal curiosity. Peter Lynch frequently illustrated this idea with examples drawn from everyday life. He invested in Dunkin' Donuts after being impressed by the product itself, before recognizing the broader growth trend behind the company. The initial insight did not come from a model, but from observation. In this sense, investment ideas can emerge from daily experience. They may also come from professional exposure or sector-specific knowledge—for example, identifying a supplier that stands out for its execution, innovation, or efficiency. Once an idea is identified, the next step is to test it. Growth characteristics must be verified to ensure the trend is real, followed by valuation analysis using tools such as the PEG ratio or portfolio tilting decisions.

It is worth noting, however, that the environment has changed significantly since Peter Lynch's time. He could observe demand directly by watching queues outside stores. Today, much of that information is also available remotely through digital signals: online reviews on Google or Trustpilot, employee feedback on platforms such as Indeed or Glassdoor, and even traffic estimates per location derived from data analytics tools. As a result, the search for mispriced small caps has become more data-rich—but also more competitive. Investors who want to pursue this approach stock by stock must now go further to maintain an informational edge, unless they choose to rely on index-based ETFs that already incorporate this exposure.

## *The* momentum

The momentum strategy is certainly the most curious. It is not based on substance at all; it's all about the trend. The idea is simple: over a period of 3 months to 1 year, what has increased significantly continues to increase significantly.

The theoretical underpinnings of this approach are less well-known than those of others. Some explain this by the fact that markets do not react immediately and that there is a delay before market participants fully integrate information. Studies have even shown that this tendency is present across all asset classes, markets, sectors, and industries. In practice, index providers such as MSCI use specific criteria to identify companies exhibiting momentum characteristics:

- The value of momentum prices over 6 months[117]= ((PT-1 / PT-7) - 1) - (Local risk-free rate);
- The value of momentum prices over 12 months[118]= ((PT-1 / PT-13) - 1) - (Local risk-free rate).

The value of each stock is calculated by combining its 6-month and 12-month performance. The method is therefore very simple. Furthermore, we have seen that the most effective way to invest in the stock market is to track it passively over the long term. Momentum fits into this logic and goes even further. It projects what has already happened into the relatively near future, hoping that it will continue a little longer for you. You want to be the last in the chain to ride the trend a little longer before selling your stock to someone who will take on this shift in momentum. **Here, you're operating on a short-term, even very short-term basis, with high volatility and rapid portfolio turnover**—not based on emotional factors, but on extremely precise indicators. **Since it was first identified in 1993, certain studies have shown that this is a significant factor**[119]**, delivering real long-term outperformance in a macroeconomic environment characterized by long cycles.** The trade-off is that volatility is constant and the risk is high, particularly during years of stock market crises when performance can be catastrophic.

John Maynard Keynes compared the stock market to a beauty contest, where the goal is not to choose the most beautiful contestant, but the one you think others will consider the most beautiful. This idea was later echoed by George Soros, who placed psychology at the center of investment decisions. Markets are often driven by fear, greed, and herd behavior[120]. In this context, investors tend to follow the crowd rather than oppose it. But the difficulty is timing: staying with the flow for too long can be just as dangerous as ignoring it entirely.

# PART VII

## Cryptocurrencies: Speculation or store of value?

# CHAPTER 22 :

## What a cryptocurrency is, and what it is not

Cryptocurrency is a digital asset that exists only in electronic form. Today, more than a thousand cryptocurrencies are in circulation, each with a market price that rises and falls according to supply and demand on trading platforms known as exchanges. These digital assets can be used for a wide range of activities over the Internet, from transferring data to making payments and moving value across the world. Unlike traditional currencies such as the U.S. dollar (USD) or the euro (EUR), however, cryptocurrencies are not issued by governments, do not exist as physical coins or banknotes, and are not backed by a central bank. As a result, their value is determined entirely by the market rather than guaranteed by a public institution.

They all rely on blockchain technology. In simple terms, a blockchain is a public digital ledger that records transactions in chronological order. Once a transaction has been added, it cannot be altered. Rather than being stored in a single location, this ledger is distributed across thousands of independent computers around the world, each holding a copy of the same records. Together, these computers form a global network. Some participants play a more active role by validating transactions[121] and ensuring that every operation follows the rules established by the protocol. This collective verification process allows the system to function without a central authority overseeing every transaction.

Because the network is decentralized, it operates continuously—24 hours a day, 7 days a week—without relying on traditional banking infrastructure. But independence from banks does not mean transactions are free. Every transaction must be processed and validated by network participants, and those participants are compensated through transaction fees[122]. These fees are typically paid in the cryptocurrency associated with the blockchain being used. For that reason, it is often useful to hold a small amount of the relevant cryptocurrency when interacting with a blockchain network.

"Cryptocurrency" is a broad term that covers many different types of digital assets. In general, it refers to assets that operate on their own blockchain[123]. bitcoin (BTC), for example, runs on the Bitcoin blockchain (with a capital letter), while ethereum (ETH) and solana (SOL) each rely on their own independent networks[124]. These are known as native cryptocurrencies because they are the assets used to power and secure their respective blockchains. Not every cryptocurrency has its own blockchain, however. When a digital asset is built on top of an existing blockchain rather than operating its own network, it is usually referred to as a token[125]. In other words, a token relies on the infrastructure of another blockchain instead of maintaining its own.

To understand whether cryptocurrencies can function as money, it is useful to return to the three traditional functions of a currency as seen previously regarding traditional currencies. First, a currency serves as a unit of account, allowing people to measure and compare the value of goods and services. Second, it acts as a medium of exchange, making it possible to buy and sell without relying on barter. Third, it is a store of value, preserving purchasing power over time. This last function is particularly important because it supports the first two.

Cryptocurrencies attempt to fulfill each of these roles. As a unit of account, a cryptocurrency can be used to express the price of a product or service. An item, for example, might cost 0.002 bitcoin (BTC), 0.056 ether (ETH), or 1 solana (SOL). In that sense, value can be measured directly in the cryptocurrency itself. As a medium of exchange, cryptocurrencies can be used to purchase goods and services. Today, some businesses accept them for online services, travel bookings, and even everyday purchases such as a cup of coffee. Their use remains voluntary, however. No individual or company is generally required to accept a cryptocurrency as payment. That privilege is usually reserved for the official currency issued by a country's central bank, which serves as legal tender and is used for taxes and most economic transactions within that jurisdiction, except where specific legislation provides otherwise[126].

The store-of-value function is where most of the debate tends to focus. The answer depends largely on the particular cryptocurrency being considered and, where relevant, the organization or ecosystem behind it. Some cryptocurrencies have characteristics that supporters believe make them effective stores of value, while others may not. For that reason, there is no single conclusion that applies to every cryptocurrency. Each must be evaluated according to its own design, purpose, and underlying characteristics.

## On the different types of cryptocurrency

Some cryptocurrencies are backed by tangible assets that exist in the real world, meaning their value depends on the collateral[127] that supports them. One of the most well-known examples is tether (USDT). **Tether is designed to maintain a value of 1 U.S. dollar (USD) per token. According to the issuing company, every USDT token created and placed into circulation is backed by at least one U.S. dollar or an equivalent asset held in reserve.** These reserves may consist of cash deposited in bank accounts or highly liquid, low-risk assets such as Treasury bills and government bonds. This backing is what allows Tether to function as a form of "digital dollar." Unlike the U.S. dollar itself, however, its value is not guaranteed by the U.S. government or the Federal Reserve, but by a private company. Another distinctive feature of Tether is that it is not limited to a single blockchain. The same token can circulate across multiple networks, including Ethereum, Algorand, Avalanche, Cosmos, Near, Polkadot, Solana, Tezos, Ton, Tron, and several others. Regardless of the blockchain used, the objective remains the same: maintaining a value close to one U.S. dollar. PayPal USD (PYUSD) follows a similar principle. Each token is intended to be worth 1 U.S. dollar and is backed by reserves held by the issuer. **What distinguishes PYUSD is its emphasis on regulatory oversight and transparency. The reserves are regularly audited by independent firms to verify that every token can be redeemed for U.S. dollars at any time.** In other words, each PayPal USD token is designed to be fully backed by dollars or highly liquid dollar-equivalent assets. The same concept can also be applied to assets other than currencies. PAX Gold (PAXG), for example, is a token whose value is linked to the price of gold. Each token represents ownership of one troy ounce of physical gold stored in the issuer's vaults in London. As a result, its intrinsic value is derived directly from the market value of the underlying gold it represents.

These examples illustrate an important distinction within the cryptocurrency ecosystem. While some digital assets are backed by identifiable assets held outside the blockchain, giving them a value directly tied to real-world collateral, others derive their value primarily from their usefulness. This is often referred to as their utility value.

Ethereum (ETH) is one of the best-known examples. At present—although technological innovation and competition may change the landscape over time—the Ethereum blockchain remains one of the most widely used blockchain networks in the world. It serves as a decentralized infrastructure on which developers can build applications, create NFTs, and deploy smart contracts. To interact with this ecosystem, users must pay for network resources using ether (ETH). As a result, the value of ETH is closely linked to the role it plays within the network. The more activity that takes place on Ethereum, the greater the demand for the cryptocurrency that powers it. The same logic applies to solana (SOL). The SOL cryptocurrency is used to pay transaction fees on the Solana blockchain. Whether a user wants to transfer funds to another person, interact with a decentralized application, or perform any other operation on the network, transaction fees are generally paid in SOL. Consequently, the value of the cryptocurrency is tied to the growth of the ecosystem. As the number of users, developers, and applications increases, demand for the cryptocurrency increases as well. This utility-based model is not limited to blockchains themselves. Many tokens derive their value from the specific services they provide within an existing platform. Consider the KuCoin Token (KCS), issued by the KuCoin cryptocurrency exchange. Holding KCS can provide benefits such as reduced trading fees, access to certain private sales, and a share of part of the platform's daily revenue distribution. In this case, the token's value comes largely from the advantages and functionalities it provides within the platform's ecosystem. Utility can also arise from solving specific technological challenges. Chainlink (LINK), for example, has become the leading provider of blockchain "oracle" services, allowing smart contracts to access data from the outside world. Other projects, such as Polkadot (DOT) and Cosmos (ATOM), focus on interoperability by helping different blockchains communicate with one another. In each case, the value proposition is linked to the problem the technology is designed to solve.

Some cryptocurrencies combine utility with scarcity. They are useful within their ecosystem, but their supply is intentionally limited in an effort to preserve value over time. Bitcoin (BTC) is the most prominent example and will be examined in greater detail in a dedicated chapter. Its value is supported by the services provided by its network—namely, the ability to transfer and store value securely through a system recognized for its high level of security. Users pay transaction fees to access this network, with those fees[128] varying according to demand and network congestion. At the same time, bitcoin's supply is capped at 21 million units, a limit that cannot be exceeded. This combination of utility and scarcity forms a central part of its value proposition. Litecoin (LTC) and Bitcoin Cash (BCH) have adopted a similar approach. Both derived from Bitcoin, were created to preserve many of Bitcoin's core principles while introducing certain technical modifications. Among their objectives are lower transaction costs and faster transaction processing, allowing users to benefit from these features without relying on additional Layer 2 solutions[129]. Like bitcoin, their value proposition rests on a combination of network utility and controlled supply.

## What this means for us

The range of possible scenarios is wide, and each calls for a different response. A few general principles can nonetheless serve as a guide. **If a cryptocurrency is backed by a tangible real-world asset and you want exposure to that asset, buying the associated token can be a sound approach. You are effectively purchasing the underlying asset in digital form—tradable on a blockchain rather than through a traditional exchange. Whether this makes sense depends primarily on the issuer's financial solidity: their ability to guarantee the value of the currency they have created. From a speculative angle, a different opportunity occasionally arises: a cryptocurrency designed to track a stable benchmark—a fiat currency, gold, silver[130]—sometimes trades below its intrinsic value. Buying at a discount and waiting for the gap to close can be profitable. The risk, however, is that the discount reflects genuine doubts about the issuer's credibility. If the issuer defaults, the market value may never recover its promised level.**

**When a cryptocurrency's value derives from its usefulness, the calculus changes again. The question becomes whether owning it serves a practical purpose that justifies the cost.** Let's imagine you love Coca-Cola and there is a Coca-Cola cryptocurrency, whose price is guaranteed by the company, each unit entitling you to a can of the brand. If a can normally costs $1, then, as a consumer, whenever the price of the Coca-Cola cryptocurrency drops below $1, it becomes worthwhile to buy it. This theoretical example applies to all cryptocurrencies that have a utility value. A real example is about solana. It allows all type of transfers on its blockchain in one to two seconds[131], at a fraction of a US cent per transaction, with near-certain execution. Using SOL to transfer USDT internationally can be considerably cheaper and faster than a conventional bank wire —not as a speculative bet, but as a practical cost-saving tool. One important caveat: unlike a banking error[132], a blockchain transaction cannot be reversed. There is no central authority to correct a mistake.

Thousands of cryptocurrencies exist for thousands of different uses. The right choice depends on your specific needs. **You must therefore choose the cryptocurrency that is most beneficial to you, based on your specific needs and criteria. You are not buying a cryptocurrency here to hold onto it, but to use it (consume it) in a smart way that benefits you. Any prediction on its potential future adoption by an even larger number of users to generate a profit is speculation—which is a legitimate activity, but one that should be entered with open eyes. That kind of bet may pay off. It may not.** Predicting the long-term value of a utility-based token is genuinely difficult, because what is useful today may be displaced tomorrow by a faster, cheaper, or more widely adopted alternative.

Beyond pure speculation, several factors shape a cryptocurrency's price over time: market trends, the yields available on certain platforms through staking or lending[133], its technological edge, and its competitive positioning relative to alternatives. Technological advancement is worth examining closely—but it should not be taken for granted. The space is young and intensely competitive. A protocol that leads today may be displaced tomorrow by something faster, cheaper, or better designed. Since long-term utility depends heavily on technological staying power. For those approaching cryptocurrency as an investment rather than a consumption tool, the preference should go to tokens that meet a genuine need, hold a defensible competitive advantage, and maintain a relatively stable circulating supply. Those three filters will not eliminate risk—but they will concentrate your exposure on the assets most likely to retain value over time, rather than those riding a trend.

# CHAPTER 23 :

## Bitcoin as the new digital gold: what the facts say

Bitcoin is today the leading cryptocurrency. It was created in 2009, in the aftermath of the 2008 financial crisis. At its origin, it can be seen as a response to traditional monetary systems, at a time when central banks were expanding money supply significantly to stabilize the financial system, support banks, and stimulate economic activity. This expansion of liquidity had the mechanical effect of diluting the purchasing power of existing monetary holdings, affecting both households and businesses. In this context, bitcoin emerged as an ideological and technological alternative. It introduced a monetary system that is digitally native and strictly limited in supply: no more than 21 million units will ever exist. This constraint is enforced by the protocol itself and, in practice, would require broad consensus across a highly decentralized network to be altered.

More than fifteen years later, bitcoin has become the dominant asset within the cryptocurrency ecosystem. It represents more than 50% of the total market value of the entire sector, with a market capitalization of around 1.5 trillion US dollars. It is often described as "digital gold," not because it is physically scarce, but because its supply is algorithmically constrained, making it resistant to discretionary issuance. Unlike traditional currencies, bitcoin does not rely on a central authority capable of adjusting supply in response to economic conditions. Its monetary policy is therefore predetermined, which is precisely what gives it its appeal to some investors and its limitations to others. Its "mining" process also plays a key role in this framework, as the creation of new units requires computational work and energy, reinforcing the perception of scarcity and production cost.

> To go further:
>
> However, the "golden" digital role" of bitcoin needs to be qualified, as the foundation of precious metals (used in crafts, jewelry, industry, dentistry, and the manufacture of medals, ingots, and coins) is much broader than that of Bitcoin. Their role and legitimacy are also far older (over 3,000 years for gold, barely 20 years for Bitcoin) and universal.
>
> On the other hand, the fact that BTC is entirely digital means there are no physical storage costs (which are expensive for gold given the metal's preciousness, and can represent anywhere from a few tenths to a few percent of the stored value each year), representing a major competitive advantage. Transportation isn't really a crucial point because gold can also be ... "tokenized" and circulate digitally around the world (or rather its title of ownership) with relatively low transaction fees.

This formal limitation protects bitcoin's value from the monetary inflation that would otherwise result from an unlimited expansion of the number of coins in circulation, which would mechanically reduce their value as supply increases. Its role is also that of a benchmark for the entire cryptocurrency universe: (1) when BTC falls, other cryptocurrencies (altcoins) often fall even more sharply; (2) some investors no longer measure performance in dollars, but in whether they hold more BTC than before; (3) pricing across the ecosystem is frequently expressed relative to bitcoin (for example, the ETH/BTC pair).

Its influence is such that some companies (such as MicroStrategy and Tether) hold bitcoin as a treasury reserve, in a manner reminiscent of how central banks historically held gold. Institutional players have also entered the space, with large asset managers and funds (such as BlackRock and Fidelity) holding significant amounts of BTC on behalf of their clients.

However, unlike a traditional currency, bitcoin is not backed by any tangible or financial asset. Its value therefore depends entirely on user demand and the collective trust of its network participants. Its key advantage, relative to conventional currencies, is that it is not tied to any single country. As a result, its value is not constrained by domestic economic tradeoffs. A traditional currency such as the Swiss franc, for example, cannot appreciate indefinitely without creating pressures on competitiveness, the current account, and domestic economic activity. These imbalances typically lead to policy responses from central banks or governments aimed at limiting excessive appreciation—constraints that do not apply in the same way to Bitcoin. In this sense, it behaves as an asset largely decoupled from national economic cycles, since it is not the official currency of any state. However, its drawback is also its defining feature. It is not linked to any state actor responsible for supporting its value in the event of a severe crisis or loss of confidence, precisely when such support might be needed most.

Calculation assumptions :

There are currently around 19.9 million bitcoins in circulation worldwide. This represents the vast majority of the maximum 21 million that will ever be created per protocol. For comparison, the money supply (M2)[134] of the US dollar is about $22 trillion. That would equate to about $1,000,000 per BTC today, in the theoretical scenario where BTC has the same monetary power as the US dollar. This assumes that it is used daily by all Americans, that approximately 88% of global trade passes through it, and that more than half (56%) of global central bank reserves are held in BTC. We are far from that. The alternative scenario, to reach this figure of one million

US dollars per bitcoin, is that, with the balance of power remaining constant, the dollar's money supply would increase tenfold (assuming a BTC price of $100,000 USD). We are also far from that. However, the M2 of the US dollar was approximately $4,667 billion in January 2000, which still represents a fivefold increase (5) in 25 years, or a growth in the US money supply of more than 6% per year over the period.

Looking at it another way, $22 trillion is also roughly equivalent to the market value of all the gold in the world. Half of that value would be tied up in jewelry. Since bitcoin is digital, it cannot meet this need, and the same is true for its industrial use. If bitcoin, considered digital gold, were to capture half the market share of investment gold or gold used as a store of value, this would correspond to a current maximum price of around $220,000 per BTC; around $145,000 per BTC for a 30% market share. Because bitcoin is not tied to any particular sector or industry, it is difficult to know the breaking point at which it would be overvalued/expensive. Its only theoretical price limit, as with all assets, is that the total value of bitcoin in circulation worldwide (market capitalization) cannot be disproportionate to the wealth produced/existing.

# PART VIII

## Building Your Asset Allocation: all things considered

# CHAPTER 24:

## The most common mistakes, and how to avoid them

*W*e were therefore able to look at the main asset classes one by one and what we can expect from them. Before concluding, it's helpful to list the most frequent mistakes. Those we observe, those we make, and those we regret. They all have in common that they almost never stem from a lack of market information, and they fall into four main categories, the principal ones being:

### Strategic errors

*What we think before we act*

- Ignoring the time horizon. Buying inflation-indexed bonds, for example, can be a good way to preserve your capital in inflationary environments, but only if you hold them until maturity. In 2022, their prices fell sharply as interest rates rose to counter the post-COVID inflationary shock. Selling in the meantime would therefore result in a loss, even if the initial calculation turned out to be correct;
- Choosing an asset based on its past performance. You don't buy an asset for its past performance, but for the role it will play in your wealth management strategy and what you can reasonably expect from it under future circumstances. Past performance provides context, not a guarantee; although price momentum may persist for a short time in the near term—what professionals call "mo-

mentum";

- Not buying your primary residence if you can't manage to save each month. You can take advantage of a stable job or particularly favorable economic conditions to embark on a real estate project and make a purchase. This will allow you to build wealth over the long term through "forced savings" generated by your monthly mortgage payments;
- Avoiding an investment simply because prices are high. Doing so may cause you to miss significant opportunities, especially when it comes to high-quality long-term investments. Over time, a high entry price tends to matter less.
- Investing all your capital at once in a single asset. A lack of diversification increases risk, and if the investment performs poorly, your entire portfolio could be significantly affected.

## Psychological errors

*How do we react when markets move?*

- Overestimating your risk tolerance. When markets are rising, risk feels abstract and losses seem purely theoretical. The reality only becomes apparent when conditions deteriorate. What would you do if your portfolio lost 20%? Or 30%? Or even more? If your answer is "sell," then it is probably not a suitable long-term investment for you. A well-constructed portfolio is one that you can hold through difficult periods. You should therefore strive to understand your true risk tolerance before investing;
- Panicking after a sharp decline in a stock's price. Once you have invested in a security, being unable to tolerate a significant downturn can be costly. Such periods may cause doubt, but selling at a loss is rarely the best solution. The same applies to selling out of relief as soon as the stock recovers to its previous level a few years later. Your caution is understandable after a difficult experience, but it is entirely possible that the investment will perform very well

after you have sold it. Over time, market cycles tend to balance out, and the impact of mistakes often diminishes;

- Trying to recover quickly after a significant loss. After a poor investment decision, some investors are tempted to take excessive risks in an attempt to make up for their losses. This emotional response frequently leads to even greater losses;
- Forgetting that holding a security is equivalent to choosing to buy it for one more day. Not selling is also a decision. If the reasons that originally justified buying an asset are no longer valid, continuing to hold it is effectively a decision to buy it again at its current price. Regularly asking yourself whether you would still buy today what you already own is one of the most valuable disciplines in investing.

## Execution errors

*How to manage your positions in practice*

- Selling everything at once after a sharp rise. Predicting the exact peak of a valuation is extremely difficult. A pragmatic approach is to sell a substantial portion of your position (for example, 70%) while keeping the remainder invested. By doing so whenever you believe it is appropriate, you lock in profits without taking the risk of being completely wrong about market timing. At the same time, you retain some exposure in case the asset continues to appreciate;
- Selling too early without a clear reason. If a stock price is rising and its fundamentals remain unchanged, there may be little justification for exiting the position. Selling simply because the price has increased often means parting with an investment that is performing well. As the saying goes, you do not kill the goose that lays the golden eggs without a compelling reason;
- Overusing leverage. Leverage allows you to invest more

than your available capital by borrowing money. While it can magnify gains, it also amplifies losses. As a result, even relatively small market movements can lead to substantial losses and, in some cases, force investors to liquidate positions at unfavorable prices;

- Maintaining a short position over the long term. Short-selling can be challenging as a long-term strategy because daily returns compound in a way that may gradually erode performance. A short position can lose value even if the underlying market does not rise significantly. For this reason, it is often preferable to diversify with assets that behave differently under various market conditions rather than rely on a prolonged bet against the market. Time generally works against long-term short positions, steadily reducing potential profits.

## The details that cost a lot

*Fees, taxes and exchange rate risk*

- Neglecting currency risk. When investing in assets denominated in foreign currencies, the performance of the underlying index is only part of the picture. What ultimately matters is the return measured in your home currency. For example, if the index rises by 5% per year but the foreign currency depreciates by 6% against your home currency, you will end up losing money despite the stock market's gains. Currency risk is often overlooked because its effects can remain invisible until they materially affect returns;
- Neglecting taxes. Many countries offer tax-advantaged investment accounts that can significantly reduce the impact of taxation (such as Roth IRAs and 401(k)s in the United States). Failing to take advantage of these vehicles can place investors at a substantial disadvantage. Over time, the tax savings can amount to significant sums, and ignoring them may substantially reduce the wealth gener-

ated by your investments;

- Underestimating fees. Brokerage commissions, fund management fees, entry and exit charges, and even transaction taxes may each appear insignificant when viewed individually. However, when compounded over twenty or thirty years, they can consume several years' worth of investment returns. This is one of the reasons why low-cost index funds have historically outperformed the vast majority of actively managed funds over the long run.

# CHAPTER 25:

## The analytical framework to adopt for making a good investment

We often talk about the risk/return trade-off. These two parameters are inseparable—but they are not symmetrical. Return depends largely on the asset itself and the economic context in which it is held. Risk depends on something more personal: the time horizon you choose, and your ability to stay the course through it.

Every asset class derives its value from a specific source. For a currency, it is the quality of the central bank's balance sheet and its ability to control inflation. For real estate, it is the capacity to generate— or save—rental income. For a bond, it is the borrower's ability to repay. For a commodity or many cryptocurrencies, it is utility. For a stock, it is the future growth of earnings. Understanding what drives value in each case is not optional. Buying an asset without understanding why it is worth what it is worth is not investing—it is guessing.

Most asset classes also have a natural time horizon over which their risk profile makes sense. The same asset can look very different depending on whether you hold it for one year, ten years, or thirty. That said, time is not a universal solvent. A cryptocurrency that is risky today may remain risky in ten years —because its risk is structural, not cyclical.

Risk is commonly defined as the possibility of not recovering your initial investment. That definition is too narrow. The real risk is becoming poorer—in any form. That includes outright losses, but also the quieter erosion of purchasing power through inflation.

Cash kept under the mattress feels safe. It is not. A price increase of just 1% per year destroys more than a quarter of your purchasing power over thirty years. In practice, inflation runs far higher: ten dollars in 1995 had the purchasing power[135] of less than five dollars by 2025. Stocks, on the other hand, can fall 20% in a matter of weeks—yet deliver a real expected return over twenty years for the investor who diversifies and stays invested. The same is true of bonds, despite the inherent risk of default.

Risk is not an absolute number. It is relative to the asset, the horizon, and the investor holding it.

| ASSET | RISK OF LOSS OF PURCHASING POWER *except in exceptional situations of hyperinflation* | | |
|---|---|---|---|
| | At 1 year old | At 10 years old | At 30 years old |
| Cash | WEAK | LOW - MEDIUM | MEDIUM - HIGH |
| Real estate | LOW - MEDIUM | LOW - MEDIUM | WEAK |
| Government bonds | WEAK | WEAK | WEAK |
| BBB bonds | LOW - MEDIUM | WEAK | WEAK |
| Gold | LOW - MEDIUM | LOW - MEDIUM | WEAK |
| Other metals | MEDIUM - HIGH | LOW - MEDIUM | LOW - MEDIUM |

| Stocks | MEDIUM - HIGH | MEDIUM - HIGH | WEAK |
|---|---|---|---|
| Cryptocurrencies | MEDIUM - HIGH | MEDIUM - HIGH | MEDIUM - HIGH |

*This refers to bonds issued by governments of the highest investment grade category. Regarding real estate, due to acquisition costs, the risk of loss on a purchase made to be resold one year later is moderate, unless the purchase price is particularly good (chapter 9), hence the "low" rating.*

A riskier investment is not automatically a more profitable one. Walking a tightrope does not generate a return — it only increases the probability of a fall. What risk demands is compensation: a higher potential gain to justify the additional exposure. The gain must be proportionate to the risk. It is never guaranteed by it.

Once you have assessed the risk, the next step is to estimate what the asset can reasonably deliver — net of all costs. Transaction fees, taxes, and indirect costs can be substantial, particularly in real estate, where acquisition costs alone can represent several percentage points of the purchase price (Chapter 9). These costs do not disappear: they extend the time needed to break even, which is why entry price and total cost of ownership matter as much as the asset's headline return. The expected return you calculate should always be based on the asset's historical performance under comparable economic circumstances.

| ASSET | ACTUAL EXPECTED EARNINGS *except in exceptional situations of hyperinflation* | |
|---|---|---|
| | *deflationary period* | *standard conditions* |
| Cash | MEDIUM - HIGH | WEAK |

| Real estate | WEAK - NEGATIVE | MEDIUM - VERY HIGH |
|---|---|---|
| Government bonds | MEDIUM - HIGH | LOW - MEDIUM |
| BBB bonds | MEDIUM - HIGH | MEDIUM - HIGH |
| Gold | WEAK - NEGATIVE | LOW - HIGH |
| Other metals | WEAK - NEGATIVE | LOW - HIGH |
| Stocks | WEAK - NEGATIVE | MEDIUM - VERY HIGH |
| Cryptocurrencies | VERY UNCERTAIN | VERY UNCERTAIN |

*Bond performance assumes diversification (Chapter 13). Normal conditions here refer to an economic environment without a major deflationary episode. In this context, the expected return on gold and equities varies depending on the circumstances: real interest rates and monetary stability for precious metals (Chapter 17); and the level of inflation and your entry point for equities (Chapter 20).*

When you bring expected return, risk, and time horizon together, one conclusion becomes unavoidable: **there is no universally best investment. There are only investments that are more or less suited to a specific situation, objective, and time frame.** The mistake is rarely in the choice of asset itself — it lies in the mismatch between the time the asset needs to deliver and the time when you will need your money. Those two horizons must be aligned before anything else.

From there, identify the economic environment you are in. Factor it into your expected return. Then look at the options that remain. Most financial decisions, once the horizon is correctly identified and the context properly read, are simpler than they first appear. The number of genuinely relevant choices narrows considerably. Let the irrelevant options fall away. You now have all the tools to make it well. All that's left is for you to make a decision. Act. And hold.

## *FINAL NOTES*

*This book could have been expanded indefinitely. We could also have included works of art, collectibles (jewelry, watches), precious stones (diamonds), exceptional wines and spirits, cars, and so on. Indeed, every item falls into a category and is potentially an asset. It is possible to invest and generate a profit regardless of the asset class. Even jeans can be purchased and then resold at a profit... they certainly made the fortunes of companies like Levi's, Lee Cooper, and Diesel. However, only the major categories of assets have been discussed here—relatively standardized assets commonly considered investment opportunities by investors. Similarly, the case of acquiring an entire company has not been discussed. This will likely be the subject of a future update.*

---

# APPENDIXES

# 1. THE HISTORICAL ORIGINS OF MONEY

The historical origins of money are remarkably diverse:

- conch shells or cowrie shells[136] (seashells) in certain societies and in many Polynesian cultures (Hawaii, Fiji, Tonga[137]); in West Africa; in India; and in Southeast Asia. They were also used in the coastal regions of China for foreign trade during the Zhou[138] Dynasty; as well as by Native American and pre-Columbian peoples in the coastal regions of the Americas;
- salt, as in the Roman Empire. Valued for its ability to preserve food and due to its scarcity. Part of soldiers' pay was given in the form of salt. Paid in this currency, which is the origin of the word "salary." The word "pay" comes from the Latin *salarium* which literally means "money for salt." Salt was also used in West Africa, where caravanners transported it over long distances across the Sahara before exchanging it for other valuable goods, such as gold, textiles, or slaves; during the Han[139] Dynasty in China, where the Chinese government instituted a salt tax system. A relatively similar system emerged centuries later in the British[140] Empire. Trade routes connecting Europe, the Middle East, and Asia facilitated the transport of salt, which was exchanged for spices, textiles, metals, and other valuable resources;
- metals. It is the physical form of money that speaks to us most today. This dates back to the 6th century B.C.,

when coins made of electrum (a natural alloy of gold and silver) were minted in Anatolia. The Greeks, Persians, and Romans widely popularized their use. Since then, this practice has continued to spread throughout the world. Paper money, in the form of banknotes, is another form of currency. A banknote[141] represents a certain amount, exchangeable for a certain quantity of metal coins. Only the medium has changed.

# 2. EXCHANGE RATE CALCULATION UNDER THE GOLD STANDARD

A fixed quantity of gold is linked to a monetary unit. To see how this worked in practice, let us consider two concrete examples:

- a *Sovereign.* The British coin had a face value of 1 pound sterling (GBP). This coin, minted between 1911 and 1925, weighs 7.99 grams and is made of 916‰ gold. It therefore contains 7.31884 grams of pure gold;
- a *Half Eagle.* The American coin had a face value of 5 US dollars (USD). This coin, minted in 1834, weighs 8.36 grams and is made of 900/1000 gold. It therefore contains 7.524 grams of pure gold.

A British *Sovereign* (1 pound sterling (GBP)) contains 7,31884 grams of pure gold; an American *Half Eagle* (5 US dollars (USD)) contain 7.524 grams, so:

1 pound sterling (GBP) contains 7.31884 grams of pure gold
5 US dollars (USD) contains 7.524 grams of pure gold

---

1 US dollar (USD) = 7.524 / 5 = 1.5048 grams of pure gold

hence

1 pound sterling (GBP) contains 7.31884 grams of pure gold
1US dollar (USD) contains 1.5048 grams of pure gold

---

1 pound sterling (GBP) = 7.31884 / 1.5048 = approximately 4.863 US dollars (USD).

Conversely, 1 US dollar (USD) = 1.5048 / 7.31884 = approximately 0.2056 British pounds (GBP).

This does not necessarily mean that one pound in the United Kingdom had the same purchasing power as 4.87 dollars in the United States at the time. Rather, it indicates that this was the official exchange rate recognized in international markets.

# 3. CALCULATION OF THE COVERAGE RATIO OF THE US FEDERAL RESERVE AND THE EUROPEAN, JAPANESE, SWISS, AND AUSTRALIAN CENTRAL BANKS

Balance sheet of the US central bank (FED)[142] as of December 31, 2024:

*figures given in billions of US dollars (USD)*

| ASSETS | | LIABILITIES | |
|---|---|---|---|
| GOLD AND CERTIFICATES | 27 | BANKNOTES IN CIRCULATION | 2,322 |
| TREASURY BONDS | 4,476 | DEPOSITS | 3,807 |
| OTHER BONDS | 2,277 | REFINANCING OPERATIONS | 888 |
| OTHER ASSETS | 288 | OTHER LIABILITIES | 51 |

The total balance sheet of the Fed is US $ 7,068 trillion (USD).

Regarding the assets:

Treasury bonds are considered to be of the highest quality, as the risk of default is regarded as virtually zero.

The same applies to the other bonds held by the Fed listed in the third row of the asset column, which correspond to mortgage-backed securities (MBS)—either (1) issued directly by federal agencies under government supervision, or (2) by government-sponsored enterprises that benefit from the "full faith and credit" of the U.S. government. This is why they almost exclusively carry an AAA credit rating (equivalent to the "high-quality" category). However, despite this rating, they are slightly less "perfect" than Treasury bonds, as they are less liquid. This means that in times of crisis, it is more difficult to sell billions of dollars in MBS than pure government debt. Similarly, there is a risk of early repayment: if people repay their loans too quickly or too slowly, the value of the security fluctuates.

As for the fourth line of the asset column, although technically equivalent to that of the U.S. government, it actually represents a claim on future cash flows guaranteed by law. Unlike a Treasury bill or an asset in the third row, this asset is not liquid. The Fed cannot sell it to absorb money. Its quality is therefore lower.

To determine the value of money in circulation, each asset category is weighted according to its quality, and all liabilities that are not money are subtracted from the total.

Calculation details:

The weighted net asset value is equal to:

[ 27 x 100% + 4,476 x 95 % + 2'277 x 80% + 288 x 0% ] - [ 888 + 51 ]
= 6,100 - [ 888 + 51 ]
= 5,161 on the one hand; while on the other hand there is 2,322 + 3'807, or 6,129 billion US dollars (USD) in the money

supply[143].

The coverage rate of the US dollar is therefore 5,161 ÷ 6,129 = 84%.

Technical explanation:

Simply put, the monetary base consists of banknotes and coins in circulation, plus the deposits that commercial banks hold at the central bank.

For a more precise calculation, on the liability side, certain deposits could have been classified as non-monetary. These include: (1) the federal government's current account with the central bank; (2) deposits from central banks and/or foreign governments; and 3) accrued pension and other post-employment benefits.

Of the $3,807 trillion in deposits held at the Fed, for example, $722 billion serves as the federal government's current account. This cannot be considered money in the strict sense because, as long as the government does not spend it, the money remains stored and does not circulate. It is economically inactive. One hundred eighty-nine (189) billion correspond to deposits from central banks and/or foreign governments. These are not dollars held by commercial banks. They do not fuel traditional interbank payments. They are used as reserve assets for these states or governments, to settle international payments, or to intervene in the foreign exchange market. Two (2) billion represent accrued pension and other post-employment benefits. These correspond to the Fed's obligations to its employees (retirement benefits, pensions, accrued employee benefits, etc.). These amounts accumulate each month in the accounts but do not circulate as money in the economy, as they are not paid out immediately. These are costs anticipated in the future, whereas the concept of risk-weighted net assets involves measuring the assets that actually back the money in circulation.

These amounts can therefore be excluded. This is money not currently in use as such. Actual money already exists and must be backed by assets, but this is not the case for sterilized instruments, which do not require such backing. Because the money does not circulate today as currency[144].

European Central Bank (ECB) balance sheet as of December 31, 2024:

*figures given in billions of euros (EUR)*

| ASSETS | | LIABILITIES | |
|---|---|---|---|
| GOLD | 872 | BANKNOTES IN CIRCULATION | 1,588 |
| BONDS IN EURO | 4,533 | DEPOSITS | 3,017 |
| FOREIGN CURRENCY BONDS | 538 | FOREIGN CURRENCY BONDS | 194 |
| OTHER ASSETS | 477 | OTHER LIABILITIES | 1,243 |

The total balance sheet of the ECB is 6,420 billion euros (EUR).

Regarding the assets:

The €4,283 trillion in euro-denominated bonds held consists primarily of eurozone government bonds (German Bunds, French OATs, Italian BTPs) and a few bonds issued by very solid private companies. The credit risk is generally very low but varies widely (since a German bond is safer than a Greek or Italian bond). Liquidity risk is low to moderate, as the ECB holds such a large share of the market that it could not sell everything at once without triggering a market crash. The remaining 250 billion consists of “other securities.” This category is often less transparent and represents investments specific to national central banks (such as the investment portfolios of the Banque de France or the Bundesbank). It includes stocks, corporate bonds, mutual funds, and sometimes slightly more exotic securities. These are not securities purchased to influence the economy, but to generate returns to cover the bank's operating costs. The risk here is higher than with monetary policy securities because these portfolios are subject to stock market volatility.

The third line of the asset column consists of €237 billion in claims on the IMF; €286 billion in bank balances and investments in securities, external loans, and other external assets, which include both highly liquid sovereign securities with virtually no credit risk (e.g., U.S. Treasuries), deposits with central banks corresponding to immediately available cash, as well as deposits with private banks—which are secure but dependent on the health of the custodian bank—and external loans, which are less liquid and cannot be sold within 24 hours to defend the currency. Of the 15 billion, 15 billion consists of claims on euro area residents denominated in foreign currencies.

As for the fourth line of the assets column, it consists of 366 billion in other assets; 20 billion in public debt denominated in euros; 34 billion in loans to euro area credit institutions related to monetary policy operations; 20 billion in claims on non-euro area residents denominated in euros; and 36 billion in other claims on euro area credit institutions denominated in euros.

Similarly, to determine the value of currency in circulation, each of these asset categories is weighted according to its quality, that is, its risk of default.

Calculation details:

The weighted net asset value is equal to:

[ 872 x 100% + (4,283 x 85% + 250 x 70%) + (237 x 100% + 286 x 80% + 15 x 90%) + (366 x 15% + 20 x 80% + 34 x 95% + 21 x

75% + 36 x 90%) ] - [ 194 + 1,243 ]
= 5,318 - [ 194 + 1,243 ]
= 3,881; whereas there is 4,605 billion euros (EUR) of money supply.

The euro coverage rate is therefore 3,881 ÷ 4,605 = 84%.

Balance sheet of the Bank of Japan (BoJ) as of December 31, 2024:

*figures given in billions of yen (JPY)*

| ASSETS | | LIABILITIES | |
|---|---|---|---|
| GOLD AND CASH | 888 | BANKNOTES IN CIRCULATION | 124,078 |
| TREASURY BONDS | 582,362 | DEPOSITS | 595,748 |
| FOREIGN CURRENCY ASSETS | 10,826 | REFINANCING OPERATIONS | 11'202 |
| OTHER ASSETS | 153,916 | OTHER LIABILITIES | 16,964 |

The total balance sheet of the BoJ is 747,992 billion yen (JPY).

Cultural note: The Bank of Japan, Japan's central bank, is listed on the Tokyo Stock Exchange. 51% of the shares are held by the Japanese government and the remaining shares are non-voting.

Regarding the assets:

The third line of the asset column corresponds to approximately 30% foreign currency deposits; 60% foreign currency securities; and 10% foreign currency loans.

As for the fourth line of the asset column, it is composed of (1) 1,407 billion in negotiable debt securities issued by companies on the money market; (2) 5,095 billion in corporate bonds; (2) 65 billion in shares; (3) 37,186 billion in exchange-traded index funds (ETFs); (4) 665 billion in Japanese real estate investment funds; 5) 108,524 billion in loans and discounted notes; the remainder being made up of other assets, largely composed of accrued interest and tax refunds, as well as buildings, land, rental assets, work in progress and other tangible fixed assets.

Similarly, to know the value of the money in circulation, each of its asset categories is weighted according to its quality, that is to say, its risk of default.

Calculation details:

The weighted net asset value is equal to:

[ 888 x 100% + 582,362 x 80% + (10,826 x 30%) x 100% + (10,826 x 60%) x 98% + (10,826 x 10%) x 85% + 1,407 x 85% + 5,095 x 80% + 65 x 30% + 37,186 x 30% + 665 x 30% + 108'524 x 90% + 974 x 65% ] - [ 11,202 + 16,964 ]
= 592,262 - [ 11,202 + 16,964 ]
=564,096; while there is 719,826 billion yen (JPY) in the money supply.

The yen's coverage ratio is therefore 564,096 ÷ 719,826 = 78%.

Balance sheet of the Swiss National Bank (SNB) as of December 31, 2024:

*figures given in billions of Swiss francs (CHF)*

| ASSETS | | LIABILITIES | |
|---|---|---|---|
| GOLD | 79 | BANKNOTES IN CIRCULATION | 74 |
| BONDS IN CHF | 4 | DEPOSITS | 420 |
| FOREIGN CURRENCY ASSETS | 754 | REFINANCING OPERATIONS | 82 |
| OTHER ASSETS | 17 | OTHER LIABILITIES | 278 |

The total balance sheet of the SNB is 854 billion Swiss francs (CHF).

Regarding the assets:

The second row of the assets column consists of 1.5 billion in bonds issued by the Swiss Confederation, its cantons, and municipalities; 2 billion in bonds issued by domestic mortgage lenders; and 0.5 billion in bonds issued by foreign companies.

The third row of the assets column consists of 522 billion in bonds; 183 billion in stocks (primarily international stocks used as invested liquidity); 19 billion in cash or demand deposits; and 30 billion in other monetary policy assets.

As for the fourth line of the assets column, it consists of 13 billion in reserve positions with the IMF and other international payment instruments; 1.5 billion in secured loans; and 2.5 billion in other assets.

Once again, to determine the value of currency in circulation, each of these asset categories is weighted according to its quality, that is, its risk of default.

Calculation details:

The weighted net asset value is equal to:

[ 79 x 100% + (1.5 x 95% + 2 x 90% + 0.5 x 80%) + (522 x 95% + 183 x 55% + 19 x 100% + 30 x 98%) + (13 x 100% + 1.5 x 85% + 2.5 x 50%) ] - [ 82 + 278 ]
= 743 - [ 82 + 278 ]
= 383; whereas there is 494 billion Swiss francs (CHF) in the money supply.

The coverage rate of the Swiss franc is therefore 383 ÷ 494 = 78%.

Australian Reserve Bank (RBA)[145] balance sheet as of December 31, 2024:

*figures given in billions of Australian dollars (AUD)*

| ASSETS | LIABILITIES |
|---|---|
| GOLD 9 | BANKNOTES IN CIRCULATION 101 |
| AUD INVESTMENTS 313 | |
| FOREIGN CURRENCY ASSETS 89 | DEPOSITS 318 |
| OTHER ASSETS 3 | OTHER LIABILITIES - 5 |

The RBA's total balance sheet is 414 billion Australian dollars (AUD).

Regarding the assets:

The third and fourth rows of the asset column consist of: (1) 56% in Australian government securities; (2) 15% in quasi-government securities; (3) 14% in AA- or A-rated bonds.

Similarly, to determine the value of money in circulation, each asset category is weighted according to its quality, that is, its default risk.

Calculation details:

The weighted net asset value is equal to:

[ 9 x 100% + (313 + 89 ) x 56% x 95% + (313 + 89 ) x 15% x 90% + (313 + 89 ) x 14% x 80% + (313 + 89 )x 15% x 50% ] - [ - 5 ]
= 352 - [ - 5 ]
= 357; while there is 419 billion Australian dollars (AUD) in the money supply.

The coverage rate of the Australian dollar is therefore 357 ÷ 419 = 85%.

Summary table:

| Cash | Weighted Net Asset Value | Money Supply | Coverage rate |
|---|---|---|---|

| US Dollars (USD) | 5,161 | 6,129 | 84% |
|---|---|---|---|
| Euro (EUR) | 3,881 | 4,605 | 84% |
| Yen (JPY) | 564,096 | 719,826 | 78% |
| Australian Dollar (AUD) | 357 | 419 | 85% |
| Swiss Francs (CHF) | 383 | 494 | 78% |

At the EUR/USD exchange rate of 1.0351[146], the ECB's weighted net assets amount to 3,881 x 1.0351 = 4,017 billion USD, for 4,605 billion EUR to be guaranteed, which means that one (1) euro is equivalent to 4,017 ÷ 4,605 = 0.87 of assets in US dollar equivalent;

The same calculation applied to the BoJ implies that one (1) yen is equivalent to 0.49 ÷ 100 of assets in US dollar equivalent[147]; that one (1) Australian dollar is equivalent to 0.53 US dollar equivalent assets[148]; and that one (1) Swiss franc is equivalent to 0.85 of assets in US dollar equivalent[149] ;

hence theoretical exchange rates EUR/USD at 0.87 ÷ 0.84 = 1.04; JPY/USD at 0.65; AUD/USD at 0.63; CHF/USD at 1.02.

<u>Summary table:</u>

| Pair | Real Price | Theoretical Course |
|---|---|---|
| EUR/USD | 1,04 | 1,04 |
| JPY/USD | 0,0063 | 0,0058 |
| AUD/USD | 0,62 | 0,63 |
| CHF/USD | 1,10 | 1,02 |

By comparing the coverage ratios of different currencies,

it is possible to estimate their relative value. However, this value is not exactly equal to the market price. It is an approximation because we are not calculating exactly the same thing here. The central bank's balance sheet reflects current conditions and serves as a record of past performance. However, an asset is also evaluated based on its future prospects and the potential return that may be generated over the long term. Among the forces that influence foreign exchange markets are:

- interest rates, which represent the return on holding currency. High interest rates attract capital and support the currency at the expense of those that offer low returns. It is indeed more advantageous to hold a currency that yields a return rather than one that yields nothing;
- inflation, which reflects purchasing power within the country. Inflation may or may not be offset by the interest rate set by the central bank. For example, at the same interest rate, if inflation is 3% in the United States and 0% in Switzerland, for example, the U.S. dollar loses its value faster than the Swiss franc in "real life." In the long run, the exchange rate is supposed to adjust to compensate for this loss of purchasing power (this is the theory of purchasing power parity (PPP)). Let's imagine that initially 1 U.S. dollar (USD) is worth 1 Swiss franc (CHF), and that a car costs 10,000 CHF in Switzerland and 10,000 USD in the United States. Over time, with inflation higher in the United States than in Switzerland, the purchasing power of the dollar declines more than that of the Swiss franc. Result: With 10,000 USD, you can no longer buy as many goods as before in the United States, whereas 10,000 CHF still allows you to buy the same car in Switzerland. In this case, it makes sense to exchange dollars for Swiss francs to preserve your purchasing power. This increased demand for the Swiss franc drives up its value relative to the dollar, until the exchange rate partially adjusts to reflect the difference in purchasing power between the two curren-

cies.

In reality, this mechanism is only partial because prices differ for several reasons.

Some costs are non-exchangeable. The price of a stuffed animal sold in a store in New York (United States), for example, incorporates the store's rent (much higher than in a rural area in Mexico), the salesperson's salary (also much higher), insurance, and electricity (partly indexed to the country's standard of living), and so on, which may explain part of the difference. Even if they were, certain services are "non-tradable". You can transport a watch but not rent, a haircut, or a medical consultation[150].

Other factors provide explanations, such as: trade barriers and transportation costs (the theory assumes there are no customs duties or quotas and that transportation is free); or that profit margins are the same everywhere (whereas companies set their prices not only based on their costs, but also on what customers are willing to pay)[151];

- the current account, which reflects trade flows (commercial power) and capital flows (financial power).

Regarding the trade balance[152] and its impact on the foreign exchange market: A country with a chronic deficit must, for example, "sell" its currency to pay for imports, which creates downward pressure. Conversely, a country with a massive trade surplus (such as Switzerland) faces the opposite situation. For a foreign customer to purchase a Swiss product, for example, they must sell their local currency to buy the exporting country's currency (the Swiss franc), which creates constant demand that naturally drives up its exchange rate, all other things being equal on the central bank's balance sheet. When both parties use the U.S. dollar (the currency most commonly used in international trade today), the principle remains the same, but another factor comes into play. The exporting company acquires these USD in exchange for its exports. However, it continues to incur costs in local currency (salaries,

taxes, rent, electricity, local suppliers, etc.), which means it is forced to sell a portion of its dollars on the foreign exchange market to buy its local currency. This constant flow of sales supports the value of the national currency. If the company keeps part of its cash in dollars for future investments in the United States, the country then becomes a net creditor, and the interest and dividends not reinvested locally flow back to the country. To be consumed locally, they must be converted into local currency, creating further upward pressure on exchange rates.
On the financial power front, the impact on a currency's value occurs to the extent that a globally renowned stock exchange attracts capital from around the world into the country, which automatically strengthens the country's currency;

- "Artificial" interventions in the foreign exchange market. These interventions are "artificial" in the sense that the central bank is acting contrary to the market's "law" of supply and demand. The value of a currency (and its relative level compared to other currencies) has numerous economic consequences for a country's economic life. When the consequences are too harmful, the central bank steps away from its role as a referee to become a market participant. It then intervenes to prop up its currency when it falls too much (which creates inflation, driving up the price of imports) and the central bank wants to halt the decline. Using its foreign exchange reserves, it sells its assets to buy back its own currency on the foreign exchange market. The risk is that it may not be strong enough against the market and that it will exhaust itself by "emptying its coffers." If it has no more assets to sell, it can no longer defend its currency. Conversely, the central bank can intervene in the foreign exchange market to weaken its currency (the most common intervention for an exporting country, as an overly strong currency makes exports more expensive). The central bank then creates domestic currency (increases its monetary liabilities) and sells it on the market to buy other assets. If the purchased assets lose value, the coverage ratio you calculate decreases. A country like Switzerland, for example, which has a huge surplus (which "pushes" its currency upward), creates money to buy foreign currencies, preventing it from rising too high and too fast;

- "Safe-haven" status and geopolitics. Where there is a market, there is psychology. Other, more political factors can also come into play in the choices made by economic actors. The U.S. dollar is the global reserve currency, and in times of crisis, everyone wants it because it is the most liquid currency (easily reusable, exchangeable, and investable). Switzerland plays, to a lesser extent, a similar role; capital constantly flows into the country because it is neutral and politically stable.

# 4. THE TURKISH CASE

To maintain the appearance of its balance sheet, the Central Bank of Turkey used currency swap transactions. Simply put, it exchanged U.S. dollars (USD) from local commercial banks for Turkish lira (TRY) that it had issued. These dollars ended up on the asset side of the central bank's balance sheet. The counterpart ended up on the liability side of the balance sheet (currency). This allowed the Turkish central bank to show "inflated" assets and reassure foreign investors who were reading its balance sheet and saw significant foreign exchange reserves there.

The problem is that the central bank's assets have been artificially "inflated" because they were based on a maturity mismatch. The danger lies less in the borrowing itself than in its duration. The central bank's liabilities (the money supply) constitute perpetual debt, whereas the assets backing them are (in part) borrowed on a very short-term basis (1- or 3-month swaps). Indeed, when money is backed by the central bank's own assets, the bank has all the time in the world to repay you with an asset representing the value of your bill. When it is financed by 1-month swaps, the situation is quite different, as the central bank is then forced to renew its dollar borrowings every month with local banks.

When, for reasons of domestic monetary policy in the United States, the Fed tightened its monetary policy, investors anticipated a rise in U.S. interest rates and decided to repatriate their dollars to the United States. As a result, they reduced dollar loans to Turkish banks, which, being short on liquidity themselves, could no longer lend them to the country's central bank.

The central bank was thus forced to return the dollars. The Turkish central bank's real net assets were thereby exposed, leading to a loss of confidence and the ensuing currency depreciation. In finance, one could say that the Turkish central bank engaged in a "reverse carry trade" at the sovereign level to mask the fragility of its own balance sheet.

What is a carry trade?

It refers to a (risky) strategy used in the foreign exchange market that involves borrowing money where interest rates are low and investing it where rates are high. You borrow a currency with a very low interest rate and exchange it for a currency that offers a high yield (such as the Turkish lira). This system works as long as the exchange rate remains stable. In the event of depreciation (a loss in value of the Turkish lira), your gain from the interest earned is wiped out by the decline in the exchange rate.

# 5. CALCULATION FORMULAS

The cost of credit is equal to:

$$\text{Monthly Payment} \times \text{Loan Term in Months} - \text{Amount Borrowed}$$

The monthly payment is equal to:

$$\frac{\text{Amount Borrowed} \times (\text{Loan Rate} \div 12)}{[\,1 - (\,1 + \text{Loan Rate} \div 12\,)\,]\text{^}(-\text{ Loan Term in Months})}$$

The amount that can be borrowed, based on the monthly payment, is therefore equal to:

$$\frac{\text{Monthly payment} \times [\,1 - (\,1 + \text{Loan Rate} \div 12\,)\,]\text{^}(-\text{ Loan Term in Months})}{(\text{Credit Rate} \div 12)}$$

# 6. AVERAGE RECOVERY RATES[153] BY YEAR

| Year of default | Weighted average |
|---|---|
| 1982 | 38.6% |
| 1983 | 56.5% |
| 1984 | 47.9% |
| 1985 | 37.0% |
| 1986 | 49.9% |
| 1987 | 51.4% |
| 1988 | 37.5% |
| 1989 | 37.9% |
| 1990 | 27.2% |
| 1991 | 34.3% |
| 1992 | 44.3% |
| 1993 | 52.7% |
| 1994 | 48.5% |

| 1995 | 49.1% |
|---|---|
| 1996 | 54.0% |
| 1997 | 54.7% |
| 1998 | 38.0% |
| 1999 | 35.1% |
| 2000 | 25.6% |
| 2001 | 31.0% |
| 2002 | 31.8% |
| 2003 | 40.2% |
| Average | 42.0% |

# 7. US BONDS ACCORDING TO THE INITIAL DEFAULT EVENT[154]

| Initial event | Weighted average |
|---|---|
| Missed principal payment | 61.4% |
| Payment default within the grace period | 54.8% |
| Securities exchange | 43.2% |
| Regulatory seizure | 38.3% |
| Late payment of interest | 26.8% |
| Bankruptcy | 31.7% |
| All events | 32.6% |

# 8. AAA BOND CALCULATION: A WORKED EXAMPLE

(reference period 1920-2008)

With

3.63% interest rate, taking an arbitrary risk-free rate of 3.00%

| Year | Average cumulative default rates |
|---|---|
| Year 1 | 0.000 |
| Year 2 | 0.009 |
| Year 3 | 0.027 |
| Year 4 | 0.082 |
| Year 5 | 0.164 |
| Year 6 | 0.252 |
| Year 7 | 0.359 |
| Year 8 | 0.514 |
| Year 9 | 0.676 |
| Year 10 | 0.863 |

1) The probability of default during the first year is 0.000%. The amount recovered is 1,000 x 55% = 550 (considering a recovery rate of 55%);
2) The probability of default during the second year is 0.009% (0.009%-0.000%). The amount recovered is 588.30 (1000 x 3.63% + 1000 x 55%);
3) The probability of default during the third year is 0.018% (0.027%-0.009%). The amount recovered is 622.60 (1000 x 3.63% x 2 + 1000 x 55%);
4) The probability of default during the fourth year is 0.055% (0.082%-0.027%). The amount recovered is 658.90 (1000 x 3.63% x 3 + 1000 x 55%);
5) The probability of default during the fifth year is 0.082% (0.164%-0.082%). The amount recovered is 695.20 (1000 x 3.63% x 4 + 1000 x 55%);
6) The probability of default during the sixth year is 0.088% (0.252%-0.164%). The amount recovered is 731.50 (1000 x 3.63% x 5 + 1000 x 55%);
7) The probability of default during the seventh year is 0.107% (0.359%-0.252%). The amount recovered is 767.80 (1000 x 3.63% x 6 + 1000 x 55%);
8) The probability of default during the eighth year is 0.155% (0.514%-0.359%). The amount recovered is 804.10 (1000 x 3.63% x 7 + 1000 x 55%);
9) The probability of default during the ninth year is 0.162% (0.676%-0.514%). The amount recovered is 840.40 (1000 x 3.63% x 8 + 1000 x 55%);
10) The probability of default during the tenth year is 0.187% (0.863%-0.676%). The amount recovered is 876.70 (1000 x 3.63% x 9 + 1000 x 55%);

And the probability of repayment at the end of the tenth year (at the scheduled maturity date) is 99.137% (100% - 0.863%). The amount recovered is 1,363 dollars (1,000 x 3,63% x 10 + 1,000).

Summing the probability-weighted recoveries across all years through maturity yields a present value of $1,358.

# 9. ENERGY PRICES

**- oil -**

Oil[155] is currently humanity's primary energy source (accounting for 30.2% of global energy demand in 2023, down from 37.2% in 1990), ahead of coal (27.8%) and natural gas (22.7%). The three leading global producers are the United States (18.9%), Russia (11.6%), and Saudi Arabia (11.2%). The main exporters are Saudi Arabia, Russia, Iraq, Canada, and the United Arab Emirates; while the main importers are China, Europe, India, and Japan.

The value of the product depends on its characteristics, density (light or heavy), purity (sulfur content), and ease of transport. The price is not uniform worldwide because it is not a uniform product. While it is not uniform, its price is nevertheless largely comparable. To put it simply, there are three (3) main benchmarks for unrefined crude oil: WTI[156] (Crude oil - WTI); Brent[157] (Crude oil - Brent); and Dubai[158] (Crude oil - Dubai). Broadly speaking, the price of a barrel of crude was $1.17 (USD) in 1917[159], before stabilizing around $3 at the end of World War II. Prices then rose sharply following the two oil crises. The first occurred in 1973 during the Yom Kippur War. An OPEC[160] embargo caused prices to quadruple in just a few months (rising from ~$3 to ~$12 per barrel), followed by a second surge when, in 1979–1980, the Iranian Islamic Revolution and the subsequent Iran-Iraq War disrupted production. Prices doubled (from ~$15 to ~$39 per barrel) before stabilizing around $20 in the mid-1980s. Oil prices rose sharply between 2002 and 2008 (from ~$20 to ~$140 per barrel), before falling dramatically to around $40 in the wake of the 2009 economic and financial crisis. Since then, it has fluctuated within a range of $20 to $120.

Note:

Technically, WTI crude oil should be more expensive because it is of higher quality. However, a barrel of Brent is often more expensive because:

- it is more mobile—it is loaded directly onto tankers, making it accessible to any buyer worldwide. The North Sea is geopolitically stable, meaning Brent prices respond more cleanly to global supply and demand signals than WTI, which is landlocked within the US pipeline network. It cannot be as easily stored in “floating storage” facilities, nor can a supertanker (VLCC[161]) be used as a mobile reservoir while waiting for prices to rise by having it remain stationary offshore (or sail very slowly);
- The settlement system is different. The U.S. crude oil (WTI) contract has a strict rule: when the contract expires, you are required to take physical delivery at Cushing, a small town in the heart of the United States. Brent, on the other hand, is often a cash-settled contract, although it can also be physically delivered.

**- coal -**

Coal[162] is currently humanity’s second-largest energy resource, accounting for 27.8% of global energy needs in 2023 (up from 25.5% in 1990), but it is the world’s leading source of electricity, ahead of natural gas (with oil being used primarily as a transportation fuel). Production is generally located where it is consumed, with three-quarters of it concentrated in three countries: China (accounting for just over half of global production and consumption), India, and the United States (each accounting for about 5% in terms of production and consumption). The major exporters in this market (producing more coal than they consume) are currently Australia, Indonesia, Russia, and to a lesser extent the United States, Canada, South Africa, and Colombia.

There are several grades of coal, each with a different price. The price varies because the "calorific value" of the coal differs depending on the deposit (and therefore often the country):

- API 2 is the reference price for imported coal (including shipping costs) in Northwestern Europe, meaning coal physically delivered to the ports of Amsterdam, Rotterdam, or Antwerp. The coal will then be used to fuel power plants and factories in Germany, the Netherlands, and Belgium. These plants constantly weigh the options of burning gas or coal. If API 2 is very low relative to the European gas price (TTF), the plants switch to coal. This makes API 2 a leading indicator of gas demand;
- API 4 is a high-quality coal with a calorific value of 6,000 kcal/kg. It is the South African benchmark (Richard's Bay), one of the most closely followed indices in the world for thermal coal (electricity). Its price reflects that of coal loaded at the port of Richards Bay in South Africa;
- API 5 is a medium-quality coal (less "pure," higher ash content, lower heat), with a calorific value of 5,500 kcal/kg. It is the Australian benchmark (Newcastle). Its price is that of coal loaded at the port of Newcastle in Australia.

### - natural gas -

Natural gas[163], now humanity's third-largest energy resource, is booming. Global production more than doubled between 1990 and 2023, as did its share of global energy production (from 19.3% in 1990 to 22.9% in 2023). The two leading producers of natural gas today are the United States (25%) and

Russia (15%), followed by Iran, China, Canada, Qatar, and Australia. Since 2017, the United States, previously a net importer, became the world's leading exporter in 2024 (18.1% of global exports), ahead of Russia (13.4%), Qatar (11.1%), Norway (11%), Australia (9.4%), and Canada (7.7%) . The European Union is a major importer (23.6%), as are China (15.5%), the rest of Europe (8.6%), and Japan (7.8%).

As for prices, they can vary significantly between regions even though the gas molecule is the same everywhere. Why such differences? Due to issues specific to transportation. Because of its inherent characteristics, the raw material is relatively immobile, resulting in relatively compartmentalized markets. This explains how it is possible for American gas (Henry Hub) to be often 3 to 8 times cheaper than European gas (TTF). Indeed, natural gas can be transported by pipeline[164] or ship:

- In the first case, once the pipeline is operational (at a cost of several hundred million or even billions of U.S. dollars), the cost of transportation is "minimal." The price of gas transported via pipeline is set for very long periods through contracts (to recoup the pipeline's construction costs). It remains stable because it does not depend on the availability of ships. Low, because they avoid costly transport by ship.
- Transporting American or Qatari gas to Europe, for example, the gas must be converted into LNG (Liquefied Natural Gas). Liquefaction involves cooling the gas to very low temperatures[165] (which is costly because it consumes a lot of energy) so that it becomes liquid. It is then transported on LNG carriers, highly specialized vessels that are therefore expensive to lease or purchase. Once it arrives at its destination (Europe in our example), it must be reheated to turn it back into gas (regasification).

Transportation costs are specific to this product. For other raw materials, such challenges do not arise, resulting in less uniform global prices. Furthermore, the war between Russia and Ukraine, which broke out in 2022, has caused major shifts in the gas market. Prices skyrocketed rapidly, and a reorganization of supply flows took place. Sanctions against Russia and the explosion of several Nord Stream pipelines supplying the European continent caused European pipeline imports to drop by half between 2022 and 2024, while imports of liquefied natural gas increased by 57% during the same period.

## - CONCLUDING REMARKS -

These energy markets are highly volatile over the short and medium term, with prices capable of falling by half in just a few months. As a result, investors must pay close attention not only to long-term trends but also to short-term market cycles.

Oil prices are currently trading at levels broadly comparable to those seen in 2006, and the same is true for natural gas. This period coincides with the rapid expansion of shale oil and gas production through large-scale hydraulic fracturing, particularly in the United States. As a result, the country has once again become a net energy exporter after more than half a century of heavy dependence on foreign imports. Investing in these markets requires monitoring both supply-side factors—such as new resource discoveries and advances in drilling technology[166]—and demand-side developments, including Covid-style lockdowns, slower economic growth, and the resulting decline in energy consumption. At the same time, prices are influenced by a wide range of other factors: logistics (shipping costs, a vessel blocking[167] a major canal, or storage facilities in Cushing reaching capacity), government policy (such as the introduction of taxes on specific energy sources or polluting industries, which directly affect profitability), and geopolitics (wars, economic sanctions, embargoes, tensions in the Persian Gulf, and OPEC decisions).

The challenge is that investors cannot remain indefinitely exposed to these commodities. The often-overlooked cost of rolling futures contracts forward gradually erodes capital—a risk that is easy to underestimate.

Paradoxically, coal—the oldest and most polluting of the three major energy sources—has experienced the strongest price appreciation over the past twenty years.

# 10. GRAIN PRICES

**- corn -**

According to the USDA National Agricultural Statistics, the price of corn has risen from US$0.77 in 1910; to US$0.69 in 1940; US$1.25 in 1960; US$3.11 in 1980; US$1.85 in 2000; US$5.18 in 2010; and is projected to be around US$4 by the end of 2024.

**- wheat -**

According to the USDA National Agricultural Statistics, the price of wheat has risen from US$0.81 in 1910; to US$0.62 in 1940; US$1.80 in 1960; US$3.90 in 1980; US$2.70 in 2000; US$6.24 in 2010; and is expected to be roughly the same price at the end of 2024.

**- soybeans -**

Soybeans[168], price has risen from US$2.92 in 1925; to US$0.81 in 1940; US$1.92 in 1960; US$6.61 in 1980; US$4.67 in 2000; US$9.86 in 2010; and US$11.03 in 2024.

These three (3) major crops (grains and oilseeds) account for the bulk of the global food market. Their combined value exceeds one trillion U.S. dollars annually. Corn is the most widely produced grain in the world (for animal feed, human consumption, and biofuels); wheat is the foundation of food security in many civilizations and thus in many countries; and soybeans are essential for industrial livestock farming and oils.

### - rice -

Rice, which feeds more than half of the world's population, can also be added to this list. However, it is an agricultural commodity that is not highly globalized in financial terms, as most of the production is consumed where it is produced, meaning that barely one-tenth of its production is traded on international markets. The number of exporting countries is limited, and prices[169] are heavily influenced by domestic policy decisions—including export bans imposed by major producers such as India, Thailand, and Vietnam.

## - CONCLUDING REMARKS -

Looking at long-term price patterns, it becomes clear that agricultural commodities are inherently cyclical markets, making them particularly attractive for shorter-term trading strategies. This behavior is largely explained by the seasonal nature of agricultural production.

The basic cycle is straightforward: plant, wait, harvest. As inventories gradually decline between harvests, supplies become tight and prices tend to firm up. By contrast, harvest season brings a surge of supply to the market. Since farmers within a given region generally harvest at roughly the same time, silos fill up quickly and prices often reach their seasonal lows. The existence of two hemispheres partly smooths this cycle, as one hemisphere is typically harvesting while the other is planting. Even so, weather remains a major source of uncertainty. Floods, droughts, hailstorms, and other adverse conditions—events that may become more frequent as climate change progresses—can severely disrupt production and amplify price swings in either direction. Agricultural markets are particularly sensitive to even small imbalances between supply and demand. A modest shortfall can trigger a sharp rise in prices, while abundant harvests can have the opposite effect. This phenomenon is commonly known as King's Law. First formalized by Charles Davenant, it describes how agricultural prices tend to react disproportionately to changes in available quantities. Because these commodities are essential to human survival, even minor disruptions in supply or demand can generate outsized price movements.

Moreover, when prices rise far above production costs, market forces often exert powerful downward pressure, eventually pulling them back toward long-term averages. Logistics and transportation also play an important role. Wars, economic sanctions, disrupted trade routes, embargoes, and blockades can all affect the flow of goods and, consequently, market prices. Speculative[170] activity further adds to the volatility.

It is also worth noting that investors seeking greater volatility may sometimes find it not in the raw agricultural commodity itself, but in downstream products such as soybean meal or soybean oil, whose price movements can be even more pronounced.

<u>On the prices of other major agricultural products</u>[171]:

**- cotton -**

Among the significant non-food commodities (although much less important than cereals in terms of volume), cotton and coffee are particularly noteworthy. The price of cotton[172] has risen from US$25.96 in 1945; to US$30.96 in 1960; US$60.48 in 1980; US$50 in 2000. It is currently around US $80 with peaks reached in 2011 (US$229) and 2012 (US$163).

**- coffee -**

While metal is metal regardless of where it is produced, the same cannot be said for agricultural products. There may be certain differences between different varieties or species.

This is the case with coffee[173]. We distinguish between Arabica and Robusta. The former has an oval-shaped bean with a wavy central groove. It is considered milder, more aromatic[174], with higher acidity and lower caffeine content than the latter. Grown at high altitudes, it is generally more expensive. Robusta, on the other hand, has a rounder bean shape and a straight central groove. It has a stronger, more bitter, earthy, or woody taste. Its acidity is lower and its caffeine content higher. Grown at lower altitudes (as it is a more resilient, hardier plant), it is generally less expensive than Arabica. The prices of both varieties move in tandem. After a series of ups and downs, they rose from 70 cents per pound in 1992 to nearly 400 cents per pound by the end of 2025 for Arabica; and from 50 cents per pound in 1992 to nearly 200 cents by the end of 2025 for Robusta.

### - cocoa -

While prices remained relatively stable in the 2000s, they have risen sharply since 2023–2024, with the price increasing more than fivefold in less than a year before gradually falling again. West Africa (Ivory Coast and Ghana) is the world's leading producer. Between 60% and 70% of the world's cocoa comes from there.

However, the region is experiencing extreme and contradictory weather conditions (a meteorological phenomenon known as El Niño). Excessive rainfall in late 2023 caused the pods to rot, followed by record-breaking heat in early 2024. The intense drought that followed "scorched" the flowers before they could develop into fruit. The result? Harvests plummeted by nearly 40% in some areas, creating an immediate physical shortage. With global reserves at an all-time low (stock shortage) and demand remaining strong, major producers and manufacturers (such as Lindt, Mars, and Nestlé) rushed to buy to secure supplies —a trend amplified by speculative fund movements. Why have prices been slowly falling since then? On the demand side, demand is stabilizing or declining due to rising prices, particularly through the sale of smaller bars[175]. On the supply side, some countries, such as Ecuador and Brazil, are gradually increasing their production to take advantage of the price hike[176]. A return to normalcy and milder weather conditions are finally calming the markets. However, another factor—one that is not seasonal —persists: a virus. The cocoa swollen shoot virus, transmitted by scale insects, attacks the trees, causing significant productivity losses. In Ghana, it is estimated that more than 80% of certain producing regions have been infected. This has created a structural (long-term) deficit that the weather alone cannot remedy. The virus has also been detected in Sri Lanka (CBSLV) and Southeast Asia (CaMMV).

## - CONCLUDING REMARKS -

First, it is worth reiterating that short- to medium-term volatility is high in these markets, and prices can move dramatically over the course of just a few months.

Second, agricultural commodities should not be viewed as a homogeneous asset class. Each market has its own dynamics, making this a field that rewards specialized knowledge. Successful investing therefore requires a careful understanding of the unique characteristics and cycles of each commodity.

Looking at the broader picture, it becomes clear that, aside from major disruptions such as climatic disasters, wars, or energy crises, agriculture throughout the twentieth century and the early twenty-first century has generally managed to keep pace with the world's growing food requirements while maintaining prices within a relatively stable range. This observation does not guarantee that the same pattern will persist in the future, but it remains a noteworthy historical fact. As a result, the long-term price appreciation of most major agricultural commodities has been relatively modest, often lagging inflation. A few notable exceptions stand out, however. Coffee prices have nearly tripled over the past fifteen years, while red meat prices have roughly doubled over the same period[177].

For investors, the opportunity lies in capitalizing on these cycles—either by participating in a sustained upward trend or by correctly anticipating exceptional events before they unfold. Neither approach is easy. As the Danish physicist Niels Bohr[178] famously remarked, "Prediction is very difficult, especially about the future."

While a favorable trend can certainly improve the odds of success, investors should bear in mind that commodity exposure cannot be maintained indefinitely without cost. Over time, the often-overlooked expense of rolling futures contracts forward can gradually erode capital. In practice, this means that being right is not enough—you also need to be right within a reasonable timeframe.

# 11. FERTILIZER PRICES

Fertilizers[179]. These products are designed to improve the growth and yield of agricultural production by providing plants with the essential nutrients for their development[180]. They are generally characterized by their NPK content[181], that are nitrogen (N), phosphorus (P) and potassium (K). This category includes: urea, phosphorus, TSP, DAP, and potassium chloride:

- Urea is the most widely used fertilizer in the world. This nitrogen-rich (N) white solid was once believed to be a product of a mysterious "vital force" that only living organisms could produce. In 1828, the chemist Friedrich Wöhler succeeded in manufacturing it in the laboratory from purely chemical minerals. This discovery now allows factories around the world to produce it[182]. Today, millions of tonnes of urea are produced each year from natural gas in industrial facilities around the world. China and India—the world's largest and second-largest producers, respectively, each with populations exceeding one billion—rely heavily on this resource and frequently impose export controls to safeguard domestic supply and prevent shortages. As a result, Russian urea—produced by either the world's third- or fourth-largest producer, depending on the year, but consistently the leading exporter —plays a dominant role in international trade. Supported by the country's vast natural gas reserves, it serves as the primary benchmark for the global market—particularly through the Urea E-Europe;
- Phosphorus (P). A raw material extracted directly from

mines, it cannot be used as is. It must be processed. Production is dominated by China, Morocco, and the United States. Morocco, however, holds by far the largest reserves in the world (approximately 70%), followed by China, Algeria, and Syria;

- TSP(P), also known as triple superphosphate, is the concentrated and processed form of the rock. It is one of the oldest and most effective phosphate fertilizers for soils that are severely deficient in phosphorus.
- DAP (N + P). It is a binary fertilizer, a mixture of nitrogen and phosphorus;
- Potassium chloride (K), often simply called potash, is a mineral salt extracted from underground mines. Canada, Russia, and Belarus are the main producers.

## - CONCLUDING REMARKS -

The fertilizer market is a highly specialized industry with a limited number of major players. These participants are consistently shaped by economies of scale and geopolitical risk. Because fertilizers ultimately underpin global food security, they carry significant strategic importance. As a result, strategic urea reserves are beginning to emerge in several countries, similar to oil stockpiles, in order to shield agricultural systems from future geopolitical shocks.

Urea is the most widely used fertilizer in the world. Russia has traditionally been one of the dominant players in this market, exporting a large share of its production due to high output and relatively low domestic consumption. The Middle East (notably Qatar and Egypt) and the United States act as a "safety valve" in the event of geopolitical tensions involving Russia. China, the world's largest producer by far, holds a particularly powerful position. It can abruptly restrict exports in order to secure supply for domestic farmers and put downward pressure on prices domestically, with major consequences for global markets. Conversely, it can reopen the floodgates and export massive volumes, sending prices sharply lower worldwide. In such scenarios, other exporters such as Qatar, Egypt, and Russia are forced to adjust prices downward in order to remain competitive.

In addition, because urea production requires large quantities of natural gas, it is naturally exposed to fluctuations in the price of its main input. On top of this geopolitical factor, it is also highly dependent on energy prices (natural gas), as is DAP, a binary fertilizer combining nitrogen and phosphorus.

We are therefore dealing with highly complex markets. These commodities are as much an investment as they are a diplomatic tool. This geopolitical dimension is also very pronounced in potassium chloride, where the number of key players is limited to just a few—essentially three, including Russia and Belarus, close allies—a phenomenon that is even more acute in phosphorus markets, with Morocco playing a central role, as is the case for TSP. We are clearly far from a stable and transparent market in which a retail investor could comfortably participate. The stakes extend well beyond that framework.

# 12. SILVER THURSDAY — MARCH 27, 1980

The Hunt brothers, wealthy American industrialists, bet heavily on the rise of silver by buying physical silver and futures positions. They used leverage (margin) and drove the price of silver up from $7.69 to $49.45 an ounce in just one year. During the last nine months of 1979, it is estimated that the two brothers controlled one-third of the world's silver supply. The situation was so critical for other professional buyers that, on March 26, 1980, the jeweler Tiffany published an article in the New York Times stating: “We find it unacceptable that anyoneaccumulatedbillions, yes, billions of dollars of silver, and thus drive prices up to such a point that others have to pay artificially high prices for silver items.”

Following intervention by regulatory authorities, the rules of the game changed. They limited new long positions and drastically increased margins, forcing the Hunt brothers to reduce their positions and inject hundreds of millions of dollars in cash to meet the margin call. Prices eventually collapsed (by 90% in two years), triggering panic on Wall Street as they were unable to meet their debt obligations and some major brokerage firms and banks went bankrupt. The Hunt brothers lost not on the underlying issues, but because exceptional measures were taken in response to the disruptions in the silver market and their consequences for market participants, thus contributing to the failure of their strategy.

# 13. THE LONDON METAL EXCHANGE (LME) NICKEL CRISIS — MARCH 2022

This episode stands in contrast to the case of the March 2022 nickel contracts on the London Metal Exchange (LME). To begin with, Tsingshan, a Chinese nickel giant, went heavily short, betting on a drop in prices. However, at the same time, the war in Ukraine triggered a panic over metal supply, and prices skyrocketed. Nickel prices nearly quadrupled in just three days. This situation forced the exchange to issue significant margin calls. The scale of these calls was such that they threatened to put 12 of its 45 clearing members in default and deplete their guarantee funds[183]. The risk of a chain reaction collapse was then very real.

In an unprecedented move, the LME decided to suspend trading and cancel eight hours of previously executed trades. Although the sheer volume of trades canceled by the LME was unprecedented, the British High Court upheld this decision after market participants challenged it in court. While this decision prevented the bankruptcy of clearing houses (whose role is to guarantee the fulfillment of these contracts by requiring collateral to cover losses), it nullified the profits of participants who had profited from the price surge and, in the process, saved the

Chinese producer.

These examples illustrate that metal futures markets are particularly volatile and risky. They also show that authorities may be compelled to unilaterally change the rules governing these markets when price movements threaten market stability or when the industrial consequences become too significant.

# 14. BUSINESS VALUATION METHODS

Numerous methods have been created. They are grouped into three main intellectual approaches:

- An intrinsic value approach. **This is the objective of the method, known as the accounting or asset-based method, which aims to calculate the net asset value (NAV).** It shows what the company would be worth if all its assets were sold at market price and all its debts were repaid at the same time. This approach aims to determine what the company is worth today, not necessarily as a cohesive whole, but as a sum of its independently valued assets. The formula is simple: it is the value of the company's assets minus its debts. In essence, this amounts to calculating equity, with the following distinction: each item in the "assets" column of the balance sheet is valued at its fair value (or actual value) rather than its book value (often recorded at the historical cost of the initial purchase price). This approach anticipates an ideal scenario, as it assumes a sale of assets under normal market conditions, without any particular panic. **It can easily give you your floor price.** For greater precision, items such as pension obligations, guarantees provided, unprovisioned litigation, deferred taxes, remaining lease payments under a finance lease, and costs of future mandatory compliance upgrades may be included. Simply put, if you buy the company for less than that amount and decide to sell it under normal market conditions, without any particular panic, you will have made a profit. The difference will be your margin. **It can go even further. The NAV can be traded at a significant discount.** The basic principle remains the same; only the terms change, so that you will no longer value the assets at their fair value but at a net asset value (i.e., with a forced-sale discount of 20 to 40% for core assets and up to 60% for inventory). Indeed, selling in a hurry is no easy task, and time pressure often forces you to sell these assets at a fire-sale price. Exit costs are added to this (closure costs, layoffs, decontamination, legal and liquidation fees, notary fees, penalties for terminated contracts, and any hidden liabilities[184]). The idea is to determine what the company is actually worth if I plan to sell it off in pieces to shut it down. From a reverse, more positive perspective, one can also ask whether the price is reasonable by considering whether it would be cheaper to build a comparable business from scratch myself, setting aside the time factor. **This is the principle of reproduction cost.** Starting again with the revalued net assets, we add all the hidden costs: training teams, obtaining regulatory approvals, building a customer base, and ramp-up time. Deferred taxes are ignored here because nothing is being sold. However, while this is easy to do for small and medium-sized businesses, it is more complicated for large ones. Indeed, how would one rebuild Coca-Cola exactly as it is? What marketing budget would be required to achieve the same brand recognition? And is that even feasible? The same applies to the company's internal know-how, which is difficult to replicate—if not entirely prohibited—because it is protected by intellectual property;

- **A comparative approach.** It involves doing what you

naturally do in real estate. When you're trying to figure out the price of an apartment you're interested in, you look at the sale prices of comparable properties in the same neighborhood. The logic is the same here, but applied to stocks. **The idea is to determine the price multiples at which the shares of comparable competitors have traded.** This basis is often a multiple (as in real estate, where a property is generally valued at X times the price per square meter[185]) of company data such as: revenue[186]; earnings before interest, taxes, depreciation, and amortization[187] (EBITDA); earnings before interest and taxes, known as operating income[188] (or EBIT); or simply net income. The earnings multiple is widely used in the stock market. It is known as the P/E ratio (Price-to-Earnings Ratio). Multiply earnings by this multiple, and you will find an estimate of your stock's value by comparison. For the three previous multiples, however, the calculation is done in two steps: first, this multiplication to determine the company's value; then subtracting financial debt to arrive at the equity value[189], which is what interests us here[190]. So, for example, if the U.S. Postal Service were to go public one day, the investment banks[191] handling the IPO would likely look at the multiples of UPS, FedEx, and DHL to determine a valuation range. We are talking about a range, not a fixed price, because the group of comparable listed companies (peer group), however good it may be, will never be identical in every respect to the company being valued, which has its own unique characteristics (growth dynamics, brand recognition, product specifics). The absence of a direct competitor (technological lead, specific positioning) thus renders the method unsuitable, due to the impossibility of linking the company to a reference group.

- A final approach, meanwhile, is based on projections of future earnings—specifically, those I can reasonably expect. Because this approach is forward-looking, it projects uncertain trajectories into the future. **The best-known of these is the discounted cash flow (DCF) method.** It involves valuing a company based on the cash flows it is capable of generating in the future. Free cash flow (FCF) is taken into account. This amount is important because it represents a sum that could potentially be distributed to the company's shareholders. We then estimate these future cash flows over the next five to ten years. For cash flows beyond the projected period, a terminal value is estimated, even if you are not planning to sell. Why? First, because without this, you cannot measure the wealth created, calculate the IRR, and ultimately compare your investments. And second, because you cannot project cash flows indefinitely. They become difficult to predict over the long term[192]. The estimated sale price (what you expect to receive if you were to sell the company at the end of your investment horizon) is often a multiple, always the same as those seen previously. The sum of all the discounted values thus gives the company's value today[193]. Because the terminal value often accounts for a large portion of this amount, your valuation is actually extremely sensitive to exit assumptions. An exit multiple of 6x versus 8x can significantly change the result. **That is why you need to make several assumptions to minimize this risk: a pessimistic, base-case, and optimistic scenario.** Not just one. Another aspect of this model is that it is based on the discounting model. That is, it assumes that a euro today is worth more than a euro tomorrow. You must therefore "discount" each future cash flow to bring it back to its present value—that is, what it can buy today and right now. However, while this model reflects the stock market's sensitivity to central bank interest rates, no one knows the exact "true" discount rate to use in practice. It is all the more difficult to determine because even a small change in the rate can drastically alter the valuation. In short, to summarize, in theory, the approach is elegant. In practice, the result depends heavily on the assumptions made (growth, discounting), which can make the valuation extremely sensitive to small changes in parameters. **It actually provides a potential value, if the promises are fulfilled.**

# 15. ANNUALIZED STOCK RETURNS BY P/E RATIO AND EARNINGS GROWTH:

| P/E Evolution | Profit growth rate | | | | | | |
|---|---|---|---|---|---|---|---|
| | -2% | 0% | 2% | 4% | 6% | 8% | 10% |
| 10 to 10 | 3.00 | 5.00 | 7.00 | 9.00 | 11.00 | 13.00 | 15.00 |
| 10 to 15 | 3.65 | 5.67 | 7.69 | 9.72 | 11.74 | 13.77 | 15.79 |
| 10 to 20 | 4.18 | 6.22 | 8.26 | 10.30 | 12.34 | 14.39 | 16.43 |
| 15 to 15 | 1.33 | 3.33 | 5.33 | 7.33 | 9.33 | 11.33 | 13.33 |
| 15 to 20 | 1.92 | 3.93 | 5.95 | 7.97 | 9.99 | 12.01 | 14.03 |
| 15 to | 2.41 | 4.44 | 6.47 | 8.5 | 10.5 | 12.57 | 14.6 |

| 25 | | | | | 4 | | |
|---|---|---|---|---|---|---|---|
| 20 to 20 | 0.50 | 2.50 | 4.50 | 6.50 | 8.50 | 10.50 | 12.50 |
| 20 to 25 | 1.01 | 3.02 | 5.04 | 7.05 | 9.07 | 11.08 | 13.10 |
| 25 to 25 | 0.00 | 2.00 | 4.00 | 6.00 | 8.00 | 10.00 | 12.00 |
| 25 to 30 | 0.45 | 2.46 | 4.47 | 6.48 | 8.49 | 10.51 | 12.52 |
| 30 to 30 | -0.33 | 1.67 | 3.67 | 5.67 | 7.67 | 9.67 | 11.67 |
| 30 to 25 | -0.79 | 1.20 | 3.19 | 5.18 | 7.17 | 9.15 | 11.14 |
| 30 to 20 | -1.32 | 0.66 | 2.63 | 4.61 | 6.58 | 8.55 | 10.53 |
| 25 to 20 | -0.52 | 1.46 | 3.45 | 5.44 | 7.46 | 9.41 | 11.39 |
| 25 to 15 | -1.15 | 0.82 | 2.79 | 4.75 | 6.72 | 8.69 | 10.68 |
| 20 to 15 | -0.11 | 1.87 | 3.85 | 5.84 | 7.82 | 9.80 | 11.78 |
| 20 to 10 | -0.88 | 1.08 | 3.04 | 5.00 | 6.95 | 8.91 | 10.87 |
| 15 to 10 | 0.61 | 2.58 | 4.56 | 6.54 | 8.51 | 10.79 | 12.46 |

Table of the annualized rate of return over 30 years, assuming a

<u>tax rate of 30%:</u>

| P/E Evolution | Profit growth rate | | | | | | |
|---|---|---|---|---|---|---|---|
| | -2% | 0% | 2% | 4% | 6% | 8% | 10% |
| 10 to 10 | 1.94 | 3.50 | 5.22 | 7.04 | 8.93 | 10.85 | 12.80 |
| 10 to 15 | 2.46 | 4.11 | 5.90 | 7.78 | 9.71 | 11.67 | 13.65 |
| 10 to 20 | 2.90 | 4.62 | 6.47 | 8.38 | 10.34 | 12.33 | 14.33 |
| 15 to 15 | 0.86 | 2.33 | 3.99 | 5.78 | 7.64 | 9.55 | 11.49 |
| 15 to 20 | 1.27 | 2.84 | 4.56 | 6.40 | 8.30 | 10.24 | 12.20 |
| 15 to 25 | 1.65 | 3.27 | 5.05 | 6.92 | 8.85 | 10.81 | 12.79 |
| 20 to 20 | 0.32 | 1.75 | 3.38 | 5.14 | 6.99 | 8.89 | 10.82 |
| 20 to 25 | 0.67 | 2.17 | 3.86 | 5.66 | 7.54 | 9.47 | 11.42 |
| 25 to 25 | 0.00 | 1.40 | 3.01 | 4.75 | 6.59 | 8.49 | 10.42 |
| 25 to 30 | 0.29 | 1.76 | 3.42 | 5.20 | 7.07 | 8.99 | 10.94 |
| 30 to 30 | -0.21 | 1.17 | 2.76 | 4.50 | 6.33 | 8.22 | 10.15 |

| | | | | | | | |
|---|---|---|---|---|---|---|---|
| 30 to 25 | -0.49 | 0.82 | 2.36 | 4.05 | 5.85 | 7.82 | 9.63 |
| 30 to 20 | -0.79 | 0.44 | 1.90 | 3.54 | 5.30 | 7.13 | 9.02 |
| 25 to 20 | -0.32 | 1.00 | 2.54 | 4.23 | 6.04 | 7.90 | 9.81 |
| 25 to 15 | -0.68 | 0.54 | 1.99 | 3.62 | 5.37 | 7.20 | 9.07 |
| 20 to 15 | -0.07 | 1.27 | 2.81 | 4.52 | 6.32 | 8.19 | 10.08 |
| 20 to 10 | -0.51 | 0.70 | 2.13 | 3.75 | 5.49 | 7.30 | 9.16 |
| 15 to 10 | 0.37 | 1.73 | 3.30 | 5.01 | 6.82 | 8.68 | 10.58 |

# 16. FREE BANKING IN 19TH-CENTURY AMERICA

According to Kevin Dowd's definition, the free banking system is a financial system that does not involve a central bank or any other financial regulator, including the government, so that financial institutions can operate freely. It was this free banking system that was in place, particularly in the 19th century in the United States.

From 1837 to 1863, the federal government withdrew almost entirely from currency management, leaving monetary freedom to each state and each private bank. During this period, depositing collateral with the state comptroller allowed one to open a bank. In return, the bank received the right to print its own private banknotes. Even though each bank printed its own currency, the gold standard remained in place, and the law required that each bank exchange its banknotes for gold or silver coins (specie) upon request. Refusing this convertibility automatically leads to the bank's bankruptcy, as its collateral is sold to reimburse customers. This free banking system results in a multitude of banknotes, theoretically of equal value (due to their convertibility into gold), but issued by different issuers.

As an economic agent (whether an individual or a business), you therefore had to pay as much attention to a banknote's face value as to its issuer, since some were more reliable than others. Since this wasn't a fixed factor over time, you had to constantly be mindful of the true value of the banknotes you carried in your pocket. To compare different banknotes, a catalog called the Bank Note Reporter existed. It showed you how far away the issuing bank was; whether the bank still existed; and whether it was considered sound. This total freedom to create money led to fierce competition among banks. A discount was applied based on distance. For example, a $1 bill from a distant bank was worth less than one from a nearby bank, because someone had to be paid to travel physically to exchange it for gold.

This system came to an end with the Civil War (1861–1865). Abraham Lincoln's federal government, needing to finance the war and stabilize the economy, created a national banknote for the first time in 1862 (the greenback, the future U.S. dollar as we know it today). In 1865, a 10% tax was imposed on all banknotes issued by private banks to compel economic agents to adopt this new national currency, which quickly gained the upper hand.

# 17. THE WINNER-TAKES-ALL DYNAMIC

In the world of technology in general, and cryptocurrency in particular, there is a "winner-takes-all" theory. This is an economic dynamic in which one or a small handful of projects capture the lion's share of value, while the majority of others remain marginal or disappear. This largely explains why Bitcoin (BTC) is now the benchmark for cryptocurrencies, even though it isn't necessarily the most advantageous. Here are the main points:

- a tendency to mimic what others are doing can occur, especially when information is uncertain, leading to a chain reaction of copied decisions, even when there are objectively good alternatives;
- availability bias. We often overestimate what is most visible and what we hear about most. Seeking out information comes at a cost, which we avoid by falling back on the options we already know;
- the fact that market participants do not necessarily analyze everything on their own. If BlackRock or Coinbase are involved in a project, there are reasons for it. They have already done the analysis for me;
- the network effect. The more users there are, the stronger the sense of utility becomes, making it even more rational for new users to join.

In summary, capital remains concentrated on the winners, and economic actors often choose the already dominant option because it seems “safer.” Investing in a small project carries a perceived higher risk. This can be explained by Prospect Theory, developed by Daniel Kahneman and Amos Tversky, which highlights that a loss is felt more intensely than a gain of the same value.

# PERSONAL NOTES

[1] Dalbar's Quantitative Analysis of Investor Behavior, published annually, shows that the average return of the individual investor is systematically lower than the market return due to those factors having as a consequence poor entry/exit timing.

[2]Insurance companies, banks, investment funds, pension funds, sovereign wealth funds.

[3]Bridgewater Associates, one of the world's largest investment funds.

[4]Or nominal bonds in English.

[5]High inflation can be advantageous for borrowers because, if the monthly payment is at a fixed rate, it remains the same while income may increase over time. In practical terms, this means that if your income remains constant (no unemployment, adjusted rents), the loan becomes less burdensome over the years. This becomes attractive, even if high inflation puts pressure on property prices in the meantime, because once the inflationary period is over, you will have acquired your property at a lower cost. On the other hand, if the purchase is made when inflation is already high, it is often accompanied by high interest rates because banks adjust to account for this situation. You therefore borrow at a higher rate initially. Hence the importance of planning ahead.

[6]Between 1% and 3% on average over the period 1870 to 2015 for most "developed" countries and in peacetime. According to: Jordà, Òscar, Katharina Knoll, Dmitry Kuvshinov, Moritz Schularick, Alan M. Taylor; "The Rate of Return on everything, 1870–2015"; Federal Reserve Bank of San Francisco Working Paper 2017-25; (2017).

[7]Source: J Benartzi & Thaler, Myopic Loss Aversion, (1995).

[8]Banknotes could then reach up to 100 trillion marks (100,000,000,000,000).

[9]The silver standard was long prevalent in certain countries, such as Mexico and the United States, which also adopted it before transitioning to the gold standard. Historically, while silver and gold have been the two most widely used primary metals, the silver standard is more prevalent in the Far East. Long before China became a centralized empire, silver was already recognized there as a medium of exchange, and its role has not diminished over the centuries. It was more and more used as a means of payment, in the form of silver ingots or banknotes (backed by silver, the metal), before becoming the true monetary standard in the country.

[10]Other assets generally consist of debt securities (loans), other currencies (foreign currencies), or cash.

[11]Other liabilities, on the other hand, are generally government deposits (the Treasury account), and deposits from credit institutions (commercial banks) with the central bank, or other bonds to credit institutions.

[12]The Chancellor of the Exchequer is the minister in charge of finance and of the treasury in the United Kingdom.

[13]One troy ounce is equal to 31.1034768 grams.

[14]Other assets generally consist of debt securities (loans), other currencies (foreign currencies), or cash.

[15]Other liabilities, on the other hand, are generally government deposits (the Treasury account), and deposits from credit institutions (commercial banks) with the central bank, or other bonds to credit institutions.

[16]Interest rates gradually decreased by 60% per year in 2002, before stabilizing at around 25% from 2006 to 2009, 15% from 2010 to 2013, and 10% from 2013 to 2016.

[17]Significant but stable inflation from 2004 to 2016, between 6% and 10% per year.

[18]This means that by law of the country, no one can refuse this currency, nor

demand to be paid in another currency. That is called legal tender. Whether it be banknotes or coins, they will be legally accepted everywhere in this zone.

[19]Initial purchase price X (1 + the annual growth rate of real estate during the period)^ the number of years of the loan.

[20]Details of the monthly payment calculation formula are in the Appendix.

[21]Source: based on data from Bloomberg L.P. and Alan D. Biller & Associates.

[22]Taxation, which may treat capital gains from real estate (primary residence) differently from income/capital gains from another source (stocks for example),

[23]Source: Jack Favilukis, Sydney C. Ludvigson and Stijn Van Nieuwerburgh. 2017. The macroeconomic effects of housing wealth, housing finance, and limited risk sharing in general equilibrium. Journal of Political Economy.

[24]Source: Jordà, Òscar, Katharina Knoll, Dmitry Kuvshinov, Moritz Schularick, Alan M. Taylor ; "The Rate of Return on everything, 1870–2015" ; Federal Reserve Bank of San Francisco Working Paper 2017-25 ; (2017).

[25]$50,000 at a rate of 3%.

[26]$80,000 at a rate of 3%.

[27]380'000 = 300'000 + 80'000

[28]75'000 = 300'000 + 175'000.

[29]Around €95,000 for a 10-year loan.

[30]Around €105,000 for a 10-year loan.

[31]In France, the Deposit Guarantee and Resolution Fund (FGDR) protects depositors in the event of the bankruptcy of a bank or authorized financial institution. It provides coverage up to €100,000 per customer and per banking institution, including all deposit accounts (current accounts, savings accounts, fixed-term accounts, etc.). The €100,000 limit applies per institution. In other words, if you have accounts at several different banks, you can be covered multiple times. In the United States, the Federal Deposit Insurance Corporation (FDIC), an independent agency of the federal government, guarantees $250,000 per depositor, per insured bank, for each category of account (individual account, joint account, retirement account, etc.). This means that, depending on your account structure, you could have more than $250,000 in coverage at a single bank if the accounts are in different categories.

[32]Although it happens, in rare cases, that some large international banks based in a country can be "stronger" than that same state.

[33]Such as the Livret A, LDDS, and LEP.

[34]Average/Satisfactory.

[35]Speculative or risky.

[36]The data relating to category A, BBB, BB, B and C bonds comes from the yieldbook Citigroup, which traces back historical spreads for the period from 1985 to 2004. Data for AAA and AA grade bonds come from Huang and Huang (2003), and refer to averages for the period from 1973 to 1993.

[37]Detailed figures are provided in the Appendix.

[38]Detailed calculation in Appendix.

[39]It is extremely rare for a company to obtain and maintain an AAA rating from major agencies (S&P, Moody's, Fitch). Only two companies worldwide consistently hold this rating, as rating agencies consider even immensely wealthy companies to present a theoretically higher risk than some sovereign states.

[40]Source: 2024 Annual Global Corporate Default And Rating Transition Study publié (2025).

[41]Companies that default have a rating trajectory that declines over time, and it is not uncommon for them to have been rated B+ a few years earlier (usually three years before default), or even BBB- (six years earlier, to put it simply) for companies in the financial sector.

[42]Source: 2024 Annual Global Corporate Default And Rating Transition Study publié (2025).

[43]Later as a percentage of household expenses.

[44]Based on the work of Ernst Engel.

[45]Based on the work of Ernst Engel.

[46]According to the work of INSEE or National Institute of Statistics and Economic Studies, a public body in charge of economic and statistical studies in France.

[47]According to the work of the U.S. Bureau of Labor Statistics.

[48]According to the work of INSEE or National Institute of Statistics and Economic Studies, a public body in charge of economic and statistical studies in France.

[49]According to the work of the U.S. Bureau of Labor Statistics.

[50]Which does not release CO2 into the atmosphere.

[51]Twice a day, major market players agree on a global reference price for gold (fixing). This is where mines sell their production and central banks obtain their supplies.

[52]This price is anchored by physical stock. The LME has warehouses all over the world, and the price displayed on the LME is for metal ready to be loaded onto a truck.

[53]A small town in Oklahoma, yet a huge oil hub and pipeline crossroads located in the middle of the US countryside.

[54]Historically, Chicago was the central hub for grain produced on the American Great Plains before it was shipped east. Today, a farmer in Ukraine or Brazil checks the prices on this marketplace before selling their harvest. It's where global price trends are determined.

[55]However, for major market players, there may be solutions that allow for remuneration for a stock of raw materials.

For gold, this is called the "gold lease rate." It's the equivalent of an interest rate. As the owner of physical gold, you "lend" it to someone else who needs it for a specific period (a jeweler or manufacturer, for example). The borrower returns the same quantity of gold plus a surplus. This surplus is the gold lease rate. This is used to generate a return on an asset that, by its very nature, does not produce any income. However, these are interprofessional market tools, reserved for professional players in the gold market:

commercial banks, investment banks, central banks, mining producers, specialized financial institutions, gold traders, and refiners. They are not accessible to individuals, small investors, or non-specialized small and medium-sized enterprises. It is therefore advantageous for the borrower to borrow gold when the "future" price is higher than the "spot" price. This situation is common because, unlike a perishable commodity (wheat, for example), gold does not expire and is easy to store. A future price lower than the current price (a situation called backwardation) is a signal of panic or extreme shortage (in this case, of physical gold).

[56]Russia and Ukraine accounted for approximately 30% of global wheat exports before the war.

[57]By disrupting maritime transport in the Black Sea and blockading Ukrainian ports, the war has caused a large portion of the world's wheat to temporarily disappear from the international market. Sanctions against Russia and logistical problems within the country are exacerbating this situation.

[58]The following year, discouraged farmers will no longer want to plant soybeans, creating a shortage... and the cycle begins again. This mechanism perpetuates and exacerbates the cycles.

[59]A quality standard imposed by the exchange. For example, the protein content of wheat or the purity of cotton. If the goods do not meet these standards, significant financial penalties may be incurred.

[60]Carrying cost refers to the cost of "holding" an asset over time before reselling it. "Holding" the asset is the total cost of owning it.

[61]Increasing liquidity (facilitates the entry of new players, avoids problems of shortage or physical surplus) to make the market more fluid on the one hand; reducing disputes over goods, risks and costs related to logistics on the other.

[62]This is what happened in 2020, during Covid, when the "future" price of oil (WTI) turned negative (-$37).

The futures contract (WTI) here corresponds to a legal obligation to physically collect the oil (in Cushing, Oklahoma). This means that you must, in practice, organize the logistics yourself to collect your barrel equivalents there. It is then up to the buyer to receive, store, refine, etc. Thus, when the futures contracts expired, traders (often financiers rather than industrialists) realized they were going to receive thousands of barrels by pipeline but had nowhere to store them. No one could physically take delivery of the oil because the storage tanks were full. The "spot" buyershaveSimply put, they refused oil, even for free, because the storage tanks were full. Hence the ensuing panic. Financiers, terrified at the prospect of taking on this burden, preferred to pay (in this case, sell at a negative price) to get rid of it and have others take it in their place. The "future" price of oil (WTI) turned negative (-$37), while the "spot" price fell sharply without ever dropping below zero.

[63]Mold for cereals, oxidation for oil, additional loss of calorific value for coal, complex and dangerous storage for gas, etc., requiring contracts to be renewed regularly in order to replicate the price.

[64]The ETF itself buys the assets (often through futures contracts). As an investor, you own a share of this fund, which itself holds these assets. The risk of loss is limited to the amount invested.

[65]It has been observed in the European market, for example, that when the price of bananas exceeds a certain psychological threshold (often 2 euros), consumers switch en masse to local, seasonal fruits like apples. This sudden drop in demand forces distributors to lower prices to clear their stock as quickly as possible. Indeed, bananas are a perishable product. If they don't sell within a few days, they spoil (turn brown), become unsellable, and are worthless, which means that you, as an investor, need to know this maximum price.

[66]These are behemoths that control immense crops but generally produce little (palm oil, sugar cane, cattle ranches). Their control over agricultural raw materials and farmers is largely due to their strategic role in storage (giant silos where farmers deposit their harvest), transport (fleets of trucks, bulk carriers, railcars), processing (corn into ethanol, glucose syrup, animal feed), and the supply of seeds and fertilizers at the beginning of the season.

[67]Gold is a dense but very ductile (soft) metal. Rare, it has been prized for its luster since antiquity. Often used in alloys, the percentage of gold it contains, called title, is recognizable by a hallmark and determined using a touchstone. The higher the fineness, the greater the quantity/percentage of gold in the alloy. 24-karat gold consists of 999‰ gold (pure gold), 22-karat gold 916‰ (22 ÷ 24), 18-karat (18K) 750‰ (18 ÷ 24), 14-karat (14K) 585‰ (14 ÷ 24), 9-karat (9K) 375‰ (9 ÷ 24), and so on.
It is primarily used in art (gilding, gold thread for textiles), crafts (jewelry, goldsmithing, medals), and to a lesser extent in industry (particularly in electronics for the manufacture of microprocessors), the production of coins and ingots (meaning that central banks now hold about a quarter of the world's gold reserves), and more marginally in dentistry (prostheses, fillings). Another significant portion of the world's gold reserves is held by Indian citizens as private savings.

[68]Silver is more common than gold. Its good malleability makes it a frequent alloying element. A 925 hallmark signifies that the silver is at least 925/1000 pure silver. Its primary use is in industry, including mechanics, nuclear power, aeronautics, biotechnology, electronics, electricity, dentistry, and more. This makes it a critical primary mineral. The remaining demand is split between purchases as a financial asset (coins, ingots, ETFs) and jewelry/goldsmithing (decorative objects, jewelry, medals). A small portion is used in photography (silver film, declining since the advent of digital photography), radiography, and food.

[69] An inverted yield curve is often a harbinger of falling interest rates. When such a decline occurs amid persistent inflation, it pushes real interest rates into negative territory. This mechanism also explains why gold can perform well before or during a recession.

[70]It is the ancient equivalent of the printing press. More than two centuries of devaluations eventually led to rampant inflation in the 3rd century after Christ. The system could no longer hold. Reforms were made (Edict of Diocletian), but to no avail. A new monetary system based on gold was then created (Constantine I[is]) to restore trust.

[71]Administrative ratio, fixed within the framework of the established monetary system, and corrected by field actors in times of crisis.

[72]Silver, relatively rare in China, is the basis of the monetary system (taxes, wages, trade), while gold serves mainly as a prestige reserve, not as everyday currency (as was also the case in the Roman Empire).

[73]Gold is rarer there. Massively exported, it enriches silver producers and leads to monetary inflation in China, a difference in value between the two metals, the driving force behind the first monetary globalization. It is because silver eventually became "too common" that nations, over time, preferred gold as the monetary standard for their currencies in the 19th century.

[74]Until 1873, the "free minting of silver dollars" existed. This meant that anyone could bring in silver (bullion or melted coins) and have it converted into dollar coins. In 1873, a law abolished this system, breaking the link and consequently reducing the demand for silver.

[75]Due to its excellent electrical and thermal conductivity, copper is used in numerous applications. It is the best electrical conductor among all non-precious metals. However, it cannot be used in overhead high-voltage power lines, where aluminum is preferred due to its lighter weight.

[76]The third most abundant chemical element in the Earth's crust, aluminum is used in fields as diverse as transportation, aeronautics, packaging, construction, and consumer goods.

[77]Including food preservation, canned goods, tableware, and other decorative items; and the production of musical instruments.

[78]Particularly in plumbing (due to its relative corrosion resistance), anti-corrosion coatings, and especially today in batteries. Also in weaponry (grenades, radiation shielding). For your information, ammunition generally consists of copper surrounding a lead core.

[79]Half of it is used to protect against corrosion via galvanizing (deposition of a thin layer of zinc on a steel or iron surface, a process used in the automotive, construction, household appliance, and industrial equipment industries, among others); and the other part for its use in the manufacture of brass, bronze, and other aluminum alloys.

[80]Through bars or coins for precious metals; and industrial plates, cathodes, or bars for other types of metals. Because prices per kilogram are often low, this can represent enormous quantities, hence the question of storage. ETFs or commodity funds are then often more advantageous because they track the price of copper or a basket of industrial metals without requiring physical storage.

[81]Source: Facts And Fantasies About Commodity Futures, by Gary Gorton and K. Geert Rouwenhorst. (2004).

[82]Financial resources (money), intellectual resources (know-how), or material resources (machinery, land, premises, business assets).

[83]Unlike an association, which is not intended to make a profit, we then say that the goal is non-profit.

[84]Because the company's articles of association may well provide for a modulation of these rights. Specific classes of shares may well exist (with voting rights, for example, but without dividend rights, with multiple voting rights, without voting rights, etc.).
[85]Little public information is available. The valuation differences between unlisted and listed companies were significant before 2008; this gap has narrowed considerably since then.
[86]What is a dividend? It's the portion of the profits that the company has made and that it decides to pay to you, as the shareholder. Not all companies have the same profit distribution policy. They have full discretion over how to allocate their profits. Some prefer to reinvest their profits to grow (often growth companies); others to buy back their own shares (to support the share price); to increase their reserves; while still others, more mature and stable, distribute them regularly.
[87]And sometimes physically close to the stock exchanges to gain a few milliseconds of information processing.
[88]Costs are proportionally lower due to the volume produced.
[89]The most well-known ones come from S&P Global-SPIVA or Vanguard. They also do the same work in the field of bonds, calculating the performance of bond funds compared to their benchmark indices, sometimes with much better results.
[90] The Costs and Benefits of Performance Fees in Mutual Funds, par Henri Servaes et Kari Sigurdsson.
[91]An S&P 500 ETF will thus replicate the trend of the S&P 500, a Nasdaq ETF the trend of the Nasdaq, a Dow Jones ETF the trend of the Dow Jones and so on.
[92]To select your ETF correctly, also look at its ability to accurately replicate the index (tracking difference), and its size, ensuring it is relatively large to guarantee both liquidity and the long-term viability of your money.
[93]With one exception over a 1-year horizon here, 64% of Brazilian managers have outperformed their index.
[94]According to The Performance of ETFs vs. Mutual Funds on the Euronext Amsterdam in the period 2010-2021, by Ana Rita de Pinho Azevedo for example, the average monthly gross performance (before management fees) was 0.8935% for ETFs versus 0.9227% for funds; and the median figure was 1.2452% for ETFs versus 1.09% for funds.
[95]MSCI ACWI represents 2,500 companies from 23 developed and 24 emerging countries.
[96]A premium of 4.4 points for the United States, compared to an average for other "developed" countries of 3.3 points observed between 1900 and 2020 according to: Elroy Dimson, Paul Marsh and Mike Staunton, Triumph of the Optimists, Princeton University Press, 2002, and Global Investment Returns Yearbook, Credit Suisse, 2021.
[97] Source: The equity risk premium: Cheap equities or expensive bonds?, par Michael Gavin, Barclays (2012).
[98] Source: Elroy Dimson, Paul Marsh and Mike Staunton, Triumph of the Optimists, Princeton University Press, 2002, and Global Investment Returns Yearbook, Credit

Suisse, 2021.

[99]This is especially true since the country has never been marked by hyperinflation, unlike other countries that have experienced it domestically (Weimar Germany, Latin America).

[100]Distribution rate close to the average of major indices, slightly higher than those practiced in the United States, but slightly lower than those of continental Europe.

[101]Because large funds, for regulatory reasons, publish their positions every quarter in the United States (with a slight delay),whenIn Europe, declarations of crossing thresholds are public (almost in real time).

[102]Listed companies are required to publish annual reports at regular intervals. Furthermore, to prevent any investors from gaining an unfair advantage, all material information (i.e., information likely to influence the share price) must be made public simultaneously to the entire market. This is known as market transparency. Thus, market data is public (company results, macroeconomic data, central bank announcements), and it is forbidden for anyone who knows it before anyone else to use it to enrich themselves before its official release. This helps ensure that everyone plays by the same rules, institutional investors and individuals alike. Otherwise, the market becomes biased and manipulated, favoring those closest to the table.

[103]Called Instant Bloomberg or IB chat.

[104]Company value calculated as follows: Market capitalization at year-end + Preferred shares + Minority interests + Financial debt - Cash

[105]Leverage which can in itself constitute a motive for investment, as for Cevian Capital, or Nelson Peltz via the Trian fund for example.

[106]Paul Singer's specialty, notably through the Elliott Management fund.

[107] Speciality of Nathan Anderson notably with the Hindenburg Research LLC funds.

[108]ROE = Earnings per share for the last 12 months ÷ Book value per share.

[109]D/E = Total Debt ÷ Book Value.

[110]Acquired amid scandalous circumstances causing the share price to plummet

[111]The company then experienced strong international growth in the context of financial globalization in the 1980s.

[112]Capacity for massive redistributions through considerable margins (revealing pricing power), massive cash reserves and recurring share buybacks.

[113]Earnings Yield = EBIT / Enterprise Value. EBIT being the operating profit and Enterprise Value: Market Capitalization + Financial Debt - Cash.

[114]ROIC = EBIT / Invested Capital. EBIT being the operating profit and Invested Capital: Equity + Financial Debt - Cash.

[115]PEG = Price-Earnings Ratio ÷ Annual earnings growth rate.

[116]S&P SmallCap 600, S&P MidCap 400 individually; or S&P Composite 1500 collectively.

[117]Value of the price "momentum" over 6 months = ((PT-1÷PT-7) - 1) - (Local risk-

free rate).
Where: PT-1 = Local price of the security one month before the reference date (T);
And: PT-7 = Local price of the security seven months before the reference date (T).
Local risk-free rates are the short-term rates in the country's local currency.

[118]Value of the 12-month price "momentum" = ((PT-1 ÷ PT-13) - 1) - (Local risk-free rate).
Where: PT-1 = Local price of the security one month before (T); And: PT-13 = Local price of the security thirteen months before the reference date (T).

[119]Sources: Elroy Dimson, Paul Marsh, and Mike Staunton, in the UBS Global Investment Returns Yearbook: Public summary edition 2026, show that the factor of momentum retrospectively offered the strongest and most persistent long-term factor performance.

[120]Howard Stanley Marks (co-founder of Oaktree Capital Management) in *The Most Important Thing.*

[121]Each operation must be approved by the network to be added to the chain. The methods used to achieve this vary depending on the blockchain used, because each has its own rules of operation. This can be done via: a "miner" (proof of work); a "validator" (proof of stake); a company/small group of authorized servers (centralized system, similar to the traditional banking system); or according to another mechanism.
Proof-of-work, notably used by blockchains like Bitcoin, Litecoin, and Monero, involves machines solving complex mathematical calculations. The first person to find the solution "wins" (called a miner), has the right to validate the block, and receives a newly created cryptocurrency (Bitcoin, Litecoin, Monero, etc.) as a reward. The system is secure but rather slow and energy-intensive.
Proof of stake, notably used by the Ethereum blockchain since 2022, but also by Cardano and Polkadot, involves validators locking (sequestering) a significant amount of network currency. A random draw is then held, and the network randomly selects a validator to approve the next transaction. The more money you have locked, the greater your chances of being chosen. This solution is more environmentally friendly and much faster than mining.

[122]These fees (transaction fees) are, for example, called "gas fees" on the Ethereum, Polygon, Arbitrum, Optimism, or BNB Chain blockchains; "network-fees"or "miner fees" on the Bitcoin blockchain, to take just these examples. They are always paid in the currency of the host blockchain, the one on which the transaction takes place and is ultimately recorded.
The term "Gas fees" refers to gas, or fuel, because that is what allows the machine to operate and execute the transaction.

[123]There are several hundred today's blockchains active worldwide.

[124]There are several hundred today's blockchains active worldwide.

[125]There are currently several thousand active tokens in the world.

[126]As in El Salvador from 2021, before the experiment ends in 2025, to comply with the conditions imposed by the IMF.

[127]The collateral is the guarantee used to protect the holder of a security, generally

against credit risks in the context of a loan or replacement in the case of a derivative transaction.

[128]Bitcoin (BTC) fees are relatively high. Each transaction is confirmed by miners, and the fees depend on network congestion and the transaction size (in bytes). Historically, they have averaged between $1 and $10 USD, and more recently, between $0.50 and $2.50 USD, but complex transactions (multiple inputs/outputs) can result in higher fees. Confirmation time is approximately 10 minutes per block.

[129]To reduce these fees, it's possible to use what's called a Layer-2 (Lightning Network). Here's the principle, which can be applied to all cryptocurrencies:
A channel is opened. Several transactions are then grouped and executed on this channel, which acts as a kind of second layer. The advantage is that the fees are lower (because they are divided and shared between several transactions), on the order of a few US cents for micro-transactions. Another benefit of this mechanism is that they can be made almost instantly.

[130] A cryptocurrency designed to remain stable against a currency (dollar, euro) or an asset (gold, silver) is called a stablecoin.

[131]The Solana blockchain can perform 1,500 to 4,000 transactions per second, theoretically up to 65,000.

[132]An insurance system exists, though less so internationally.

[133]Staking yield is the return obtained by staking an asset.cryptocurrencyto participate in the operation of a blockchain network. This factor directly influences the price, potentially temporarily overriding fundamentals, as with a"traditional" currency".

[134]The money supply (M2) of the US dollar: aggregate of banknotes and coins in circulation; demand deposits of central banks; individuals and businesses; term deposits of less than 2 years; and savings accounts less than USD 100'000.

[135]Knowing the correspondence between USD values over time can be calculated or found directly via websites that use official inflation data for the country.

[136]Cowrie shells.

[137]Shells, called "pa'akai", were used there as a means of exchange in local trade and for rituals.

[138]Around 1046-256 AD.

[139]Around 206 BC-220 AD.

[140]Its place was so prevalent in the Indian Empire that the salt march led by Mahatma Gandhi in 1930 to protest against the British tax on salt and colonial control had a considerable impact.

[141]Paper money was invented around the 7th century by the Tang dynasty in China. It was then backed by silver, the metal that became the true monetary standard in the country. This is what is known as the silver standard.

[142] The Federal Reserve.

[143]Also called central bank money.

[144]The calculation would then give 6,100 - [888 + 51 + 722 + 189 + 2] = 4,248; for 2,322 + 3,807 - [722 + 189 + 2] = 5,216 billion US dollars (USD) of money supply, i.e. a

coverage rate of the US dollar of 81%.

[145] Reserve Bank of Australia.

[146]Daily Currency Exchange Rates Notice from U.S. Customs and Border Protection dated December 31, 2024.

[147] At the JPY/USD exchange rate from the U.S. Customs and Border Protection Daily Currency Notice of December 31, 2024, of 0.0063.

[148] At the U.S. Customs and Border Protection Daily Currency Notice AUD/USD exchange rate of December 31, 2024 of 0.6185.

[149] At the CHF/USD exchange rate of 1.1027 from the U.S. Customs and Border Protection Daily Currency Notice dated December 31, 2024.

[150]That's the Balassa-Samuelson effect.

[151]This is called "pricing-to-market".

[152]The trade balance is the difference between what a country sells (exports) and what it buys (imports).

[153] Source: Recovery Rates on Defaulted Corporate Bonds and Preferred Stocks, 1982–2003, Moody's (2003).

[154] Source: Recovery Rates on Defaulted Corporate Bonds and Preferred Stocks, 1982–2003, Moody's (2003).

[155]A natural liquid which, once refined, allows the production of various fuels, such as gasoline, diesel, gases (butane, propane) and various combustibles. Its exploitation is one of the pillars of industrial economies, as petroleum provides almost all liquid fuels (gasoline, fuel oil, diesel, kerosene, LPG) while naphtha (a transparent liquid, a mixture of hydrocarbons resulting from the distillation of petroleum) produced by refining is the basis of the petrochemical industry, from which a very large number of common materials are derived (plastics, synthetic textiles, synthetic rubbers, detergents, adhesives, fertilizers, cosmetics, etc.). The heavier fractions lead to bitumen (used for similar/complementary purposes to concrete, particularly for sidewalks, parking lots, terraces, port facilities, airports), paraffins (for leather lubrication, waterproofing, sealants and paints, insulation for submerging electrical equipment, manufacturing of firelighters for barbecues, candles, explosives or smoke bombs mixed with potassium nitrate), and lubricants of all kinds.

[156]This is the benchmark crude oil for the United States. Of excellent quality (light and smooth, with low sulfur), it is the easiest and cheapest to refine into gasoline. Its price is set in Cushing, Oklahoma, a major pipeline hub in the heart of the US. This means that, in practical terms, you logically have to go there to get it to benefit from this price.

[157]Brent crude (from the North Sea) is slightly less "pure" than WTI, but it remains a high-quality oil (light and smooth), ideal for diesel and gasoline. Even at sea, it can be loaded directly onto tankers for shipment worldwide, making it an important benchmark.

[158]Dubai (Dubai Fateh). It comes from the Fateh oil field (offshore oil production area). Of average quality (more viscous, "acidic" with a high sulfur content, and corro-

sive), it requires more complex refining. However, it is a Persian Gulf oil that is immediately available for purchase.

[159]1,17 dollars in 1917 would be equivalent to approximately thirty dollars today.

[160]The Organization of the Petroleum Exporting Countries (OPEC) is an intergovernmental organization of countries that negotiate on all aspects of oil production, its price, and future concession rights. Its 12 members (Algeria, Gabon, Libya, Nigeria, Equatorial Guinea, Republic of the Congo, Venezuela, Saudi Arabia, United Arab Emirates, Iraq, Iran, and Kuwait), acting as a cartel, agree on the quantity and price of oil exported.

[161]VLCC stands for Very Large Crude Carrier. These are giant oil tankers, so heavy (between 200,000 tonnes and 400,000 tonnes) that they cannot pass through the Suez Canal (except with lightning), nor through the Panama Canal, and must pass through the major capes.

[162]It is a black or dark brown rock, rich in carbon, extracted from underground or open-pit mines depending on the location. Older than petroleum, its extraction made the Industrial Revolution possible from the 18th century onwards. Often called coal, it should be distinguished from charcoal, which is not a rock, but rather made from wood.

[163]Natural gas is a gaseous mixture consisting mainly of methane that is found in nature, particularly in oil fields, gas fields and coal seams. It is extracted by drilling and is used as a fuel (domestic and industrial heating, electricity production in gas-fired power plants, vehicle fuel) as well as an industrial raw material (hydrogen production, synthesis of plastics, ammonia useful for the production of fertilizers because it is a molecule that contains nitrogen (N) assimilable by plants, as well as other chemical products).

[164]Gas pipeline or pipeline in English.

[165]-162°C (-259.6 °F) for methane (natural gas/LNG)

[166]Large-scale hydraulic fracturing, horizontal drilling for example for shale gas.

[167]Like the Ever Given, which became stuck in the Suez Canal for six days following an incident. Those few days were enough to create a massive traffic jam of over 400 ships, single-handedly halting 10% of global trade.

[168]per bushel according to the USDA National Agricultural Statistics Service for farmers in Iowa.

[169]A different price applies between Thai rice 5% (up to 5% broken grains), Thai rice 25% (up to 25% broken grains), Thai rice A1 (almost 100% broken grains), or Vietnamese rice 5% (usually the cheapest of the four).

[170]From a farmer who is trying, for the survival of his farm, to know what the best production will be for next year, whether it is a multinational trading company, or a simple speculator.

[171]It contains wheat, corn, rice, barley, sorghum; soybeans, soy flour, soybean oil, peanuts, peanut oil, fishmeal, coconut oil, palm oil, palm kernel oil; "beverages" such as cocoa, coffee, and tea; bananas, beef, chicken, lamb, oranges, shrimp, sugar; wood

with logs, plywood, sawn timber; other raw materials such as cotton, or rubber; and so on.

[172] per pound.

[173]Fruity, floral, chocolatey

[174]This is not the only example. Tea, to name just one, follows a similar logic. The price generally differs between Colombo (the most expensive), Kolkata, and Mombasa (the least expensive).

[175]A phenomenon called "shrinkflation", or reducing quantities while keeping the price intact (or increasing it to a lesser extent) to lessen the negative effect perceived by the consumer.

[176]Within the limits imposed by nature, because the growth of a cocoa tree takes longer than that of an ear of corn, hence the different timeframes.

[177]Livestock (cattle sold on the Chicago Mercantile Exchange) no longer involves physical delivery. The exchange has switched to financial settlement.

[178]Niels Henrik David Bohr (October 7, 1885 – November 18, 1962) is known for his contribution to the development of quantum mechanics, for which he received numerous honors, including the 1922 Nobel Prize in Physics.

[179]Fertilizers have been used since ancient times. On the soil of agricultural land were, for example, widespread: phosphates from bones, nitrogen from manure (from cows for example), potassium from ash (from volcanoes for example).

[180]There are (1) organic fertilizers (of animal or plant origin to put it simply); (2) mineral fertilizers (the nutrients are mineral salts, obtained by extraction and/or by industrial/physical/chemical processes); and (3) organo-mineral fertilizers (with nutrients of both organic and mineral origin, obtained by mixing and/or chemical combination).

[181]Three numbers separated by hyphens, for example 18-51-20. In France, for example, fertilizers are all products in which one of the major element contents exceeds 3%.

[182]Mainly Chinese (world's leading producer with about 30% of production), Indian (world's second largest producer) and Russian (world's third or fourth largest producer, but leading exporter).

[183] Working paper 24-09, Central Clearing and Trade Cancellation : The Case of LME Nickel Contracts on March 8, 2022, John Heilbron. Office of Financial Research.

[184]For example, for disputes, customer guarantees, or tax risks.

[185]Before refining the estimate by taking into account the specific characteristics of the property (interior layout, work to be done, monthly charges, energy consumption, terrace or not, possible view, neighborhood).

[186]ARR or Annual Recurring Revenue in English.

[187]EBITDA is widely used because it masks, at least partially, differences in financial structure and accounting practices. Warren Buffett frowned upon it, pointing out that ignoring depreciation can create an overly optimistic picture. However, it does allow for calculations to be performed when EBIT is negative.

[188]Operating profit = net income + net interest expense + taxes paid.

[189]Only financial debt, and not operating debt, is considered, as the latter is part of the normal business cycle, and multiples such as those used for revenue, EBITDA, or EBIT already value it assuming a normal level of working capital. Therefore, this is already "included" in their market valuation.

[190]Let's imagine, for example, that a company makes 10 billion dollars of revenue and that the multiple is 2. The company's value will be 20 billion dollars (2 x 10). However, this will not be the equity value of the shares.
Financial debt must be deducted from this. If it is, let say, 5 billion dollars, the total value of the shares will then be 15 (20 - 5). This intermediate step is important regarding the multiples of revenue; recurring annual revenue; EBITDA; and EBIT. However, this second manipulation is not necessary for the P/E ratio (Price/Earnings Ratio) or the Price/Book ratio (Price/Book Ratio). These multiples are already...cleanliness"in their construction.

[191]Like Goldman Sachs, BNP Paribas, or Morgan Stanley.

[192]With the exception of companies with full order books, selling through long-term contracts or subscriptions, for example (contractual cash flows). This is the case, for instance, in infrastructure such as airports or highways operated under concessions, pipelines, or port terminals. It is also the case in the energy sector when projects are long-term.

[193]Then subtract the financial debts again to arrive back at the value of the securities (equity value).